Praise for *Je*

This book is terrible—as in terribly timely, helpful, challenging, insightful, and *needed* today! Yes, you've read other books on money. No, you've *never* read a book like this—or in all my years I haven't. Counterculture isn't just a phrase. It's the message of this book—and of the "terrible" advice Jesus Himself gives us that is terribly needed in your family and mine. Read this book and give a copy to your adult children as well!

JOHN TRENT
Gary D. Chapman Chair of Marriage and Family Ministry and Therapy, Moody Theological Seminary; president, StrongFamilies .com; author of *The Blessing* and *LifeMapping*

I've spent most of my professional career interacting with CPAs who understand earthly accounting principles. Few of them can explain heavenly accounting concepts with such wit and wisdom. Read this book and you won't just learn why Jesus talked about money so much. You will be equipped for trustworthy service that is neither corrupt nor negligent.

DAN BUSBY
President, Evangelical Council for Financial Accountability (ECFA)

Combining the professional expertise of an accounting professor with the astute judgment of a careful Bible student, John Thornton gives us a perceptive and practical analysis of the countercultural and counterintuitive teaching of our Lord about how we should view and use money. In addition to being helped by recognizing how Jesus' counsel flows from His mission to glorify His Father, readers will also appreciate the candor with which the author shares his own journey in assimilating this divine wisdom (illustrating that while the path of obedience is not easy, it is always worth it!).

RANDAL ROBERTS
President and Professor of Spiritual Formation, Western Seminary, Portland, OR

Martin Luther famously spoke of the "three conversions necessary to every man: the head, the heart and the purse." But few have so eloquently explained how those three conversions inform and draw from one another. And that's why I love this book. Written by a thoughtful, disciple-making, accountant-turned-professor, this book will challenge you to not only think about, but actually put into practice, what Jesus says about money. And as it does, it will take a direct shot at what matters the most—your heart. Read this book; you'll be glad you did.

RYAN T. HARTWIG
Author, *Teams That Thrive: Five Disciplines of Collaborative Church Leadership*

An insightful and thought-provoking book about Jesus' teaching on the topic of money. With his background as both an accountant and a college professor, John Thornton provides a special perspective in addressing this important topic.

JIM CANNING
Former VP/CFO, World Vision Int.

Some of us go to God with our agenda and ask Him to "sign here." In this book, John takes an honest and insightful look at how we should view money and the impact it can have in our daily walk. Reading this book will challenge you to follow Christ with everything, including your bank account, and John does it in an unassuming way that everyone can relate to. Be prepared to give up your agenda!

Vonna Laue
Managing Partner, CapinCrouse, LLP

In a society where money too often determines status and worth, John's fresh, poignant, and witty exploration of his own journey and how it intersects with Jesus' terrible financial advice reveals a deep personal commitment to following Christ and His principles regardless of the cost. Intensely practical and applicable, this book is a must-read for both the "haves" and the "have nots," as it redefines wealth and recasts an understanding of stewardship in light of the gospel. As you read, prepare to be convicted; expect to be changed.

Jill Hartwig
Mom, wife, educational specialist

Clear, practical, and definitely biblical in a subversive way. I found myself uncomfortably exposed. Far too often I allow money to master me. I both love money and fear money and in doing so, I subtly trade in the true God for a false one.

Norm Schwab
Pastor, Northview Bible Church, Spokane, WA

I found the book very inspirational and thought-provoking, so much so that I plan to read it again soon.

BONITA K. PETERSON KRAMER
Professor of Accounting, Jake Jabs College of Business & Entrepreneurship, Montana State University

Are you concerned about a financial crash? As an Air Force pilot, I was trained to know that under certain conditions and blinded by weather I could be upside down in my plane and not know it with tragic consequences. The only way to know my true reality and status was to depend on my flight instruments and not my feelings. Perhaps modern financial advice is upside-down. That is what John Thornton is telling us; we need to depend on God to know our true status and be safe. Check it out and avoid a financial crash.

JIM WOODY/USAF RETIRED
Former Vice Dean and Permanent Professor of Management, USAF Academy

This book is truly inspired! I laughed and cried as John shared his journey through the uncomfortable truths of Jesus' words. Thanks for helping me stay focused on the right Master!

BRUCE FITZGERALD
Realtor, Kirkland, WA

Jesus' Terrible Financial Advice

Flipping the Tables on Peace, Prosperity, and the Pursuit of Happiness

JOHN THORNTON

MOODY PUBLISHERS

CHICAGO

Edited by Connor Sterchi
Interior Design: Ragont Design
Cover Design: Faceout Studio

Library of Congress Cataloging-in-Publication Data

Names: Thornton, John (CPA), author.
Title: Jesus' terrible financial advice : flipping the tables on peace,
   prosperity, and the pursuit of happiness / John Thornton.
Description: Chicago : Moody Publishers, 2017. | Includes bibliographical
   references.
Identifiers: LCCN 2016041474 (print) | LCCN 2016046426 (ebook) | ISBN
   9780802414861 | ISBN 9780802494795
Subjects: LCSH: Wealth--Religious aspects--Christianity. | Money--Religious
   aspects--Christianity. | Wealth--Biblical teaching. | Money--Biblical
   teaching.
Classification: LCC BR115.W4 T47 2017 (print) | LCC BR115.W4 (ebook)
   | DDC
   241/.68--dc23
LC record available at https://lccn.loc.gov/2016041474

We hope you enjoy this book from Moody Publishers. Our goal is to provide high-quality, thought-provoking books and products that connect truth to your real needs and challenges. For more information on other books and products written and produced from a biblical perspective, go to www.moodypublishers.com or write to:

Moody Publishers
820 N. LaSalle Boulevard
Chicago, IL 60610

3 5 7 9 10 8 6 4 2

Printed in the United States of America

To Alyssa, love of my life,
and our sons Joshua, Benjamin, and Jacob

Contents

Preface

There are some things in life that money just can't buy. Big things. Like purpose. But for everything else, there's money. Yet most Christians are confused about it. And no wonder! Two thousand years ago the Son of God sat down on the side of a mountain to teach one of the most oppressed people the world has ever known. The large crowd assembled was hoping against hope that He had come to rescue them. Imagine their disappointment when He opened with the words "Blessed are the poor . . ."

How could they be blessed? You can almost hear the crowd's collective groan. He was off to a terrible start.

But here's a news flash for you. Jesus meant to be terrible.

Terrible. Webster defines *terrible* as "strongly repulsive," but also, "very shocking and upsetting," and "formidable in nature."[1] The root word is *terror*, from which we get *terrific*, *terrifying*, and *terrible*. I invite you to listen to Jesus' financial advice again, or for the first time, and see just how terrible it is.

What we believe about money matters. As a CPA with a

PhD in accounting, I know money. Practically, philosophically, personally, and professionally. This book is a firsthand account of questions I've wrestled through over the past twenty years, questions every Christian must answer. But despite spending most of my life working with money, I relied on just one rule while writing this book: "If my theology disagrees with God, one of us is wrong, and it's not Him."

Why? Because what we believe about God matters even more. What we *really* believe, not what we say we believe. There is no better example of this than Daniel, my favorite accountant in the Bible. Three times he rose to number two in the kingdom, and he was an advisor of the Babylonian and Persian empires. Why? Because even evil kings want someone who is "trustworthy and neither corrupt nor negligent" (Dan. 6:4) watching over their stuff. Daniel served these kings well because of what he believed about God. That God is sovereign over the kingdoms of the world. But Daniel isn't my favorite accountant in the Bible because he rose to the top of these kingdoms. He's my favorite accountant because two of those kings changed their edict from "Worship me only," to "Worship Daniel's God only." (Go to gettingrichright.com for more of the story.)

Do you really want to live a life that matters? If God can use an accountant to save the world twice, He can use you as well.

1

The Book
I Couldn't Write

*"Father, the hour has come. Glorify
your Son, that your Son may glorify you."*

JOHN 17:1

ifteen years ago, as a young accounting professor at the US Air Force Academy, I sat down to write a book about God's perspective on money. And I knew exactly what I wanted Him to say.

Don't judge me. It's not like I was going to put words in His mouth. Quite the opposite, really. I was intent on using the Bible as my sole resource, despite my somewhat unique position of holding a PhD in accounting in addition to years of practical experience as a CPA. I even think my heart was in the right place. I'd seen a lot of friends and family—whether rich or poor—struggle with money, and really wanted to help. Besides, I had an unbelievable story to tell of God's provision, and I thought it needed to be told.

Early in our married life, my wife, Alyssa, and I had left professional careers for graduate school. I was a CPA and Alyssa was an actuary (they specialize in the mathematics of probability). According to the *Wall Street Journal*, accountants invented actuaries so there would be someone more boring than themselves. So we were the original fun couple.

Our goal in returning to school was to free up time to live more meaningful lives. I planned to become an accounting professor to free up summers for youth ministry. And as we put God first, He provided for us beyond our imagination. Though our budget required that we give up over 80 percent of our income and live on an income at just half of the US poverty level, we not only survived—we thrived! After six years of grad school we were debt free, and we'd gone to Disneyland, Disney World, and Maui three times.

But wait—there's more! We also had two sons along the way, and Alyssa was able to stay home and focus on them. And instead of going bankrupt, our net worth doubled over those lean years. By putting God first and combining some simple accounting tools with a few basic biblical principles, we'd made it through the desert and were headed to the Promised Land.

As a new professor at the Academy, I polished my talk—"Who wants to be a millionaire?"—on cadets, showing them how, by following a simple plan, they could invest just $2,000 per year for seven years after they graduated, and without ever investing another cent, retire a millionaire. (If the suspense is killing you, you can visit my website, gettingrichright.com, for a short explanation of how.)

That's the book I planned to write. Because what Alyssa and I did wasn't a miracle. It was mundane. And the difference is important. You can plan for the mundane, but not for miracles.

The Blind Side

Spring break, April 2000. That's when God blindsided me—four years after completing my doctorate in accounting and ten years after becoming a CPA. I had recently read through the entire Bible and highlighted every passage I could find on wealth. So that week I completely immersed myself in the topic by typing every highlighted verse into a Word document. By midweek I had over 1,300 passages on 115 pages. Single-spaced, 12-point font. Then I classified them into twenty-three categories.

What I found was remarkably different than what I expected.

That week I penned the following:

April, 2000
Book
Eeoww! I just spent the last two days typing into
my computer every passage I could find in the New
Testament on wealth, and I stand convicted. It's
not that I haven't read the Bible before. In fact,
I've read portions of it most every day for decades,
and in the last couple years read the entire Bible,
specifically highlighting every passage I could find
related to wealth. No, when it comes to the Bible,
you'd have to classify me as well read. But it was
in my actions of the past week that caused me to
react with what can be described as equal parts
conviction, consternation, confusion, dread, and
excitement. . . . And as I stand at the crossroads,
I'm scared. God, increase my faith.

Jesus' Terrible Financial Advice

Pleased that my own financial plan had come together so well, imagine my dismay when I found the following advice from Jesus: "And if anyone wants to sue you and take your shirt, hand over your coat as well" (Matt. 5:40).

Huh? In case you missed it, let me tell you straight up that this is terrible financial advice. And on so many levels! Obviously Jesus didn't grow up in America. We love to sue people! It's our national pastime. Who hasn't heard of the woman who spilled her coffee leaving a McDonald's drive-thru, sued for millions—and won! Coffee she was holding in a cup between her legs. Apparently the cup didn't say that the contents were hot. Duh! What kind of coffee did she think she was getting? That's the only kind of coffee they sold back then. So not only did McDonald's cough up the big bucks, they now have to print on all their cups: "Warning: Contents are hot!"

What could Jesus have in mind by giving His disciples that kind of advice? If someone wants to sue you, let him?

And His follow-up was even worse.

"Give to the one who asks you" (Matt. 5:42).

Did He mean *everybody*? I'd be broke in a week! Why not buy my wife the shirt "I'm with Stupid!", add a big tat to my forehead that confirms it, and stand on the street corner with a stack of $50s until the carnage is complete?

Wanting to remain true to my original intent of showing what God says about money, I decided to avoid explaining away Jesus' words, and instead keep an open mind while I typed on. Besides, it was still Monday morning, and I was only on the third passage. To cover myself, I opened a second screen in Windows and started recording all the questions that came to mind.

"Give to the one who asks you."
1. Could I give to the wrong person? Surely it matters who I give to? Shouldn't I use some judgment on this?

2. Could I give too much?
3. Could I give irresponsibly? What about people who have dependents? Should they give to everyone who asks? I have three small sons, for goodness' sake! And a wife. It's one thing if I ruin my life, but what about theirs?

Switching back to the main screen, I returned to typing in passages of Scripture on wealth. But all I seemed to be getting was more and more of the same from Jesus.

"But when you give to the needy, do not let your left hand know what your right hand is doing, so that your giving may be in secret" (Matt. 6:3–4a).

Does that go for my left brain as well as my right? Perhaps if my logical, sequential, rational, analytical, objective left brain didn't know what my random, intuitive, holistic, subjective right brain was doing, I'd find Jesus' advice more palatable.

On the upside, Jesus did follow up His advice with some hope: "Then your Father, who sees what is done in secret, will reward you" (Matt. 6:4b).

Still, those rewards sounded pretty distant, and I was reeling from too many right hooks to the head to be overly comforted.

Then came the knockout blow. After telling me, "Do not store up for yourselves treasures on earth" (Matt. 6:19), He followed it up with this statement: "No one can serve two masters. Either you will hate the one and love the other, or you will be devoted to the one and despise the other. You cannot serve both God and money" (Matt. 6:24).

Bam! For several minutes straight Jesus had taken off the gloves, and that was the blow that put me down for the count. It's not like I hadn't heard that verse before. I've heard sermons on it. And I'd probably read it a hundred times. But with all the other questions swirling around in my mind that morning, this time it knocked me flat.

Love God but despise money? I must have missed something, because I didn't see the connection. Why couldn't I enjoy both? Money is a blessing. I could think of several rich people in the Bible who loved God. Job, Abraham, David. And hadn't God provided for us in a spectacular fashion?

So what was I missing?

The Purpose-Driven Son

In a word: *purpose*.

Jesus' purpose, that is.

This answer is so stark, so blatant, so obvious, that it seems impossible to miss. Yet I was guilty of doing what every person has done when coming to Jesus, from the first encounters recorded in the Gospels to the present day. I came with my agenda. My needs and wants. Just like many of you.

What do you want, or need, from God?

Start a list, if you'd like. Is there one thing? Or a thousand?

Regardless of length, our lists are precisely why we miss

Jesus' true purpose in coming to earth. Because He meets everyone who comes to Him exactly where they're at.

But thankfully, He doesn't leave us there. Instead, He redirects us to His Father.

Jesus' sole purpose on earth was to glorify His Father.

Yes, Jesus came "to destroy the devil's work" (1 John 3:8) by ending the curse brought on creation by the fall.

JESUS' purpose is the foundational truth that unlocks everything He teaches about money. Indeed, all His teachings hinge on understanding His purpose in coming to this earth.

Yes, Jesus came to give us life, and life to the full.

Yes, Jesus came to set us free from death and bring us home.

Yes to all of God's promises to us. "For no matter how many promises God has made, they are 'Yes' in Christ. And so through him the 'Amen' is spoken by us to the glory of God" (2 Cor. 1:20). But these are all a part of His overarching purpose: *to glorify His Father.*

By *glory*, I mean the adoration and accolades rightfully due the person who performed the praiseworthy deed. Our God is one. What He does reflects who He is. And He is "the LORD, who exercises kindness, justice and righteousness on earth, for in these [He] delight[s]" (Jer. 9:24).

Jesus came to restore a true picture of who His Father is. Ever since the fall, when we listened to the serpent disparage God's true character, sin has blinded us from clearly seeing the Father for who He really is.

Jesus fully reveals the mystery of His purpose in His final prayer on the night He gave up His life for ours.

> "Father, the hour has come. Glorify your Son, that your Son may glorify you. For you granted him authority over all people that he might give eternal life to all those you have given him. Now this is eternal life: that they know you, the only true God, and Jesus Christ, whom you have sent. I have brought you glory on earth by finishing the work you gave me to do. And now, Father, glorify me in your presence with the glory I had with you before the world began." (John 17:1b–5)

Jesus' purpose is the foundational truth that unlocks everything He teaches about money. Indeed, all His teachings hinge on understanding His purpose in coming to this earth.

TRUTH:

Jesus' sole purpose on earth was to glorify His Father.

Everything He did and everything He said was to show us His Father. Of course, He did many other things here on earth, but they all fit under this main purpose. People came to Him with their sick and their sin, their dying and their dead, and Jesus met them where they were. He met their needs and felt their pain. And through it all, He redirected them *from* what they thought they needed *to* what they really needed—His Father.

More often than not, they had money problems. Whether they knew it or not. Just like us.

After all, "money is the answer for everything" (Eccl. 10:19), in that it is the common denominator we use to measure our hopes and dreams. So it shouldn't surprise us that many of Jesus' teachings relate to money.

And it shouldn't surprise us that some of Jesus' teachings on money are hard. Hard in the sense that they are often at odds with what the world teaches. In fact, they are often at odds with what the *church* teaches. So hard, that we discard them. Or Him.

John records a time when, after a particularly hard teaching, many of His disciples turned back and no longer followed Him:

> "You do not want to leave too, do you?" Jesus asked the Twelve.
>
> Simon Peter answered him, "Lord, to whom shall we go? You have the words of eternal life. We have come to believe and to know that you are the Holy One of God." (John 6:67–69)

Like Jesus' early followers, we are at a crossroads. He flips the tables on everything we thought we knew about peace, prosperity, and the pursuit of happiness. Jesus' teachings about money and wealth hit us where we live, shake us free from a life that leads to death, and leave us immeasurably more blessed than we ever imagined. All with the single-minded purpose of bringing glory to His Father.

SOME of Jesus' teachings on money are hard. Hard in the sense that they are often at odds with what the world teaches. In fact, they are often at odds with what the *church* teaches. So hard, that we discard them. Or Him.

Jesus rips our hearts and minds open, exposing our deepest desires and greatest fears.

That's where money had me fifteen years ago. Fearful. And like so many of His early followers, my response was, "Lord, increase my faith." I was at a crossroads I didn't know existed, where the blessings of right living intersect with God's plan for my life.

Financial guru Dave Ramsey has tapped into our deeply felt need to get control of our money with his tagline "live like no one else now so later you can *live* like no one else." But only in Jesus do we find the answer to the last half of that statement.

This book uncovers the truths Jesus taught to live a life that matters. And it all starts with aligning our purpose with His. To live a life that brings glory to God.

What will you do with Jesus' terrible financial advice?

2

Epiphany

*"Why do you call me, 'Lord, Lord,'
and do not do what I say?"*

LUKE 6:46

Return with me to April 2000—spring break at the US Air Force Academy—when I was typing every biblical passage I could find on wealth into a Word document. With Jesus' teaching staring me in the face, I couldn't avoid the obvious question.

Did He really mean it?

And I wondered what it would look like if we did what He said.

Every once in a while I have an epiphany. No, not a revelatory manifestation of a divine being. I'm not seeing anything physical. I like to use the word "epiphany" when I'm reading God's Word and have an "aha" moment—when I see something clearly for the first time.

My great epiphany came as a graduate student at Washington State University when I was asked to speak at a Good Friday service for one of the college ministries on campus. I always try to say yes to these invitations, as it is refreshing for an accountant to get to talk about things that really matter.

On this particular occasion, Alyssa and I were also involved in a young couples' Bible study, led by Bruce, a PhD student in agricultural economics. Bruce and Cindy (not their real names) had committed their lives to sharing the gospel in countries where others couldn't get in, and Bruce wanted a degree that would open doors to those places. Something that was really needed.

We were using the inductive method of studying the Bible. Induction, as used in the field of logic, is a principle of reasoning to a conclusion by looking at specific cases to see if there is a general rule to be discovered. That is, reasoning from the particular to the general.

Our purpose in using this method to study the Bible was to let the individual passage speak for itself. We have a natural tendency to explain away teachings that are hard to understand with ones that we do understand. In doing so, we run the danger of missing a truth in the present passage we're reading by moving to other passages found in Scripture. Worse yet is the habit of adding our personal or cultural baggage to try to explain why God doesn't, or can't, mean *that*.

We were working our way through the gospel of Luke, and to give us each a chance to apply the inductive method, the group rotated leaders. As it happened, Bruce had assigned me to lead that week. We were in Luke 6, one of Jesus' most famous sermons, where He tells His disciples,

> "Love your enemies, do good to those who hate you, bless those who curse you, pray for those who mistreat you. If someone strikes you on one cheek, turn to them the other also. If someone takes your coat, do not withhold your shirt from them." (Luke 6:27–29)

At this point, Jack Cooney, a new finance faculty member just done with his doctoral work, asked, "So if somebody takes my mountain bike, I'm supposed to just let him have it?"

To be straight up, I'll tell you that Jack was one of those guys who always asked questions I couldn't answer. Jack was the most educated guy I'd ever met. In addition to a PhD in finance, he also held a law degree, and was a CPA. When it came to learning, he was pathological. He was so enamored with education that while delivering their fourth child a few months earlier, Jack became intensely interested in the doctor's post-delivery work, causing his wife, Teresa, to sit up in the surgery and blurt out, "Jack! Don't even think about medical school!"

Jack had a way of asking the obvious questions that somehow I could never get right. I'm pretty sure if he asked me, "How's the weather?" I'd get it wrong. It was his unusual way of thinking that led to one of the most embarrassing events in my life, my dissertation defense five years later, where he dropped in to view the proceedings, was given the chance to ask the first question, and I promptly passed out. But I digress . . .

Jack's question about whether he should just let some guy take his mountain bike, which by the way was his daily transportation to work, led to a lively group discussion. But by the end of the evening we hadn't come to a consensus. I closed the night down by saying, "I don't know. I'm sure there must be some other passages about justice and such, but if we're going to do this 'inductive' Bible study thing, we can't just throw out Jesus' words."

We agreed to think about it and take up Luke 6 again the next week.

All this was in the back of my mind as I prepared to speak at a Good Friday service for a student group on campus later that week. As was my usual custom when I spoke on a topic, I tried to read as much about it as possible. In this case, all four Gospels recount Jesus' crucifixion, so there was no shortage of perspectives. To be really prepared, I read all four renditions of the account, which can be found in Matthew 26:57–27:56, Mark 14:53–15:47, Luke 22:63–23:49, and John 18:12–19:30.

As I tried to distill down all that happened that Good

Friday, I saw that on the night Jesus was betrayed, He was taken to the three major ruling bodies of his day—the religious rulers, the Roman government, and the secular Jewish government. He was mocked, spit on, and beaten to within an inch of His life. At the cross, the soldiers stripped Him naked and divided His clothes into four piles, then cast dice for His underwear, a seamless garment whose value they didn't want to destroy.

As Jesus hung there, thirsty and gasping for air, He managed to not only provide care for His mother and invite a thief to paradise, but in the midst of sneering rulers, mocking spectators, and greedy soldiers, pray, "Father, forgive them, for they do not know what they are doing" (Luke 23:34).

And at that moment, I had an epiphany. My "aha" moment.

When Jesus' words from our Bible study collided with His actions at the crucifixion, I saw what I'd never seen before. I saw that Jesus meant what He said.

When Jesus told His disciples back on that mountainside, "If someone slaps you on one cheek, turn to them the other also," He meant it. And not the way I thought He meant it. I thought He meant, "Be the bigger man. Walk away."

I've been slapped really hard twice in my life. Once by Alyssa when we were dating. Boy, did I deserve that one. Rather than being gallant, I walked right out her front door. While it was closed. Both the door and the accompanying wood-framed screen door shattered to pieces. Not my finest hour.

The second slap came as a young camp counselor, when a silly girl slapped me upside the head for no apparent reason. I did better with that one. I shook it off and walked away.

That's what I thought Jesus meant when He said, "Turn the other cheek."

YET while we are drawn to Jesus, amazed by His teachings that He fully backed by His actions, we shrink in fear that He would expect the same from us.

But Jesus meant so much more. He meant to turn the other cheek again and again and again. Before the high priest and the Sanhedrin. Before Pilate and the Roman soldiers. Before Herod and his soldiers.

And when those soldiers were casting dice for His underwear at the foot of the cross, He showed what He meant by "do not withhold your shirt" to the one who had just stolen your coat. He took His teaching all the way down to the last stitch.

Finally, as Jesus' life ebbed away, He used one of His last breaths to say, "Father, forgive them, for they do not know what they are doing" (Luke 23:34). And I saw how Jesus had included that in His earlier teachings to His disciples as well:

> But love your enemies, do good to them, and lend to them without expecting to get anything back. Then your reward will be great, and you will be children of the Most High, because he is kind to the ungrateful and wicked. Be merciful, just as your Father is merciful. (Luke 6:35–36)

Suddenly, I saw what I'd never seen before. In essentially the same order as the words He spoke to His disciples on the mountainside, He took those ideals to their extreme on the cross. From "turning the other cheek," to being beaten nearly to death; from "let them take your shirt as well," all the way down to letting them cast dice for His undergarment; from "give to the one who asks you," to giving eternal life to a criminal who only a while before had been hurling insults at Him. And finally, offering forgiveness to all of them. Even those who didn't ask for forgiveness.

This is what separates Jesus and His teachings from all others. When it was time to put everything on the line, Jesus showed that He didn't just talk a good game. He lived it. To the full.

On Good Friday, Jesus showed what He meant by His teachings. He showed that He meant them completely. This is a core truth about all of Jesus' teachings, including those about money.

TRUTH:

Jesus meant every word He said.

In this He stands alone. By living every word He taught, Jesus justified His claim, "When I am lifted up," referring to His upcoming crucifixion, "[I] will draw all people to myself" (John 12:32). People tell me that they don't believe in all those hocus-pocus miracles that Jesus supposedly performed. To me, when I read Jesus' teachings, they are miracles in and of themselves. In my role as chair of Professionalism and Ethics for the American Accounting Association, I've had nearly twenty years to study the best philosophers of the present and the past. Yet Jesus' words are far beyond anything I've ever heard. To the postmodern world, Jesus is our apologetic.

Yet while we are drawn to Jesus, amazed by His teachings that He fully backed by His actions, we shrink in fear that He would expect the same from us. The practical realities of walking His talk paralyze us with fear and bring us crashing back down to earth. Instead, we shrink back. Like Peter, we want to walk on water but can't see Jesus through the waves.

Regardless of how far we take it, how could that kind of advice help us get out of debt? Or save for retirement? How could Jesus' teachings lead to peace or prosperity, let alone happiness?

So instead of putting His words into practice, I looked for exceptions. Qualifications. What are the scenarios where Jesus' teachings wouldn't hold?

We love to play out the hypothetical. What would it look like if somebody took Jesus' ideas to the extreme? That's really what Jack was asking, when he brought up his mountain bike.

So, what would it look like if you follow Jesus' terrible financial advice?

In a worst-case scenario, you might look a lot like Him.

3

A Tale of
Two Masters

"You cannot serve both God and money."

MATTHEW 6:24c

For over a dozen years, I stopped writing this book. I wanted to write with integrity, but I couldn't get past some of the terrible, or terrifying, things Jesus said. Above all, the one verse I couldn't get over was this: "No one can serve two masters. Either you will hate the one and love the other, or you will be devoted to the one and despise the other. You cannot serve both God and money" (Matt. 6:24).

So, what is Jesus' hang-up with money? And why can't I love them both?

I'll tell you straight up, I love God. Not because I'm so good, but because He is. God loved me first, and loves me best.

I've known that God loves me most my life. But the true depth of God's love is something that grows on you. Sometimes slowly, and sometimes in great bursts.

The starkest of these moments came to me as a young graduate student, after Alyssa had given birth to our first son, Joshua. Naturally, we loved him deeply. When he was twenty-two months old, we took him and the grandparents to a WSU football game, and afterwards back to the student lounge to have dinner and hang out. As we ate pizza, Joshua chased a ping-pong ball around the table in the way that gives toddlers that label.

In his speedy romp, just as he was about to corral the ball, Joshua gleefully ran full-on into the corner of the ping-pong table, striking his head exactly at the height of his right eye. And that quickly, he was knocked flat.

I dropped my pizza and ran to pick him up, expecting an imminent scream. But instead, Joshua just lay in my arms. His eyes were wide open, but rolled so far back that all I could see was the whites of them. Everyone was frantic. Time slowed down. Someone called 911.

As the seconds relentlessly turned to minutes, Josh faded to that sickly shade of blue that tells you life is draining away. And as I held him, I cried out to God, "Please don't take my son. I'd miss him too much."

Then, in an instant, as quickly as it started, it ended. Josh began to sob. His eyes returned home and his color came back. We heaved a sigh of relief as the paramedics rushed in and carried us away to the emergency room.

That night, we woke Josh at regular intervals to check for a concussion by flashing a light into his pupils to make sure they were dilating properly. And in one of those moments, as I was holding him in my arms and rocking him back to sleep, praising God for returning him to me, I was struck by the depth of God's love for me.

Earlier that day I would have given anything to have my son back. But it was outside my power to act. Yet God, who had the power to save His Son, didn't. He gave Him up to save me.

God's love is amazing. So nothing is going to shake my conviction to love Him—heart, soul, mind, and strength (see Mark 12:30). Where Jesus got me was the part about hating the other master, Money.

Why can't I love them both?

The truth of Jesus' teaching here is key to understanding His perspective on wealth. But instead, we try to explain away the power of Jesus' words. Because Jesus wasn't just talking in hyperbole, saying that you should love God so much more than money that it's as if you hated money itself. And He wasn't saying that it is wrong to be rich. Or even that money itself is bad. He meant so much more than that.

Glory Theft

To understand what Jesus was saying about God and money, you have to look back at the history of God's chosen people. Back to the time of the prophet Jeremiah, 655–586 BC, who for forty years, during the reigns of five kings, forewarned the tribe of Judah that God was going to bring down horrific curses on His people. Curses God had promised through Moses more than seven hundred years earlier, that even the "most gentle and sensitive woman among you—so sensitive and gentle that she would not venture to touch the ground with the sole of her foot," would eat her own children (Deut. 28:56–57).

Despite Jeremiah's repeated warnings and prophecies, the people refused to turn from their sins. In the war-torn years that followed, God's curses annihilated most of Israel and culminated in a seventy-year sentence of captivity for the survivors under two ruthless, godless kingdoms.

What sin would cause a loving God to so harshly discipline His chosen people?

Idolatry.

Through Jeremiah, God pointed out the many grievances He had against His people, from their mistreatment of the poor, fatherless, and widows, to their greed, fatness, and self-indulgence. But the sin of idolatry rose far above them all. That sin caused God to pour out a double-measure of His wrath.

In God's own words, "I will repay them double for their wickedness and their sin, because they have defiled my land with the lifeless forms of their vile images and have filled my inheritance with their detestable idols" (Jer. 16:18).

God, in His amazing love, had taken them out of a brutal slavery to the Promised Land. Yet His chosen people had traded Him in for the idols of those they had conquered. And because of it, God repeatedly warned them that He was going to give them a double-measure of His discipline.

> "When you tell these people all this and they ask you, 'Why has the LORD decreed such a great disaster against us? What wrong have we done? What sin have we committed against the LORD our God?' then say to them, 'It is because your ancestors forsook me,' declares the LORD, 'and followed other gods and served and worshiped them.'" (Jer. 16:10–11)

If you're like me, you probably don't think a lot about idols. Idols are, like, the Stone Age. Or maybe somewhere in Africa. They certainly don't impact my world. No big deal, right?

Yet they are very big deal to God. So big that not one, but two, of the Ten Commandments are devoted to them. And the first two at that. "You shall have no other gods before me" and "You shall not make for yourself an image in the form of anything in heaven above or on the earth beneath or in the waters below" (Ex. 20:3, 4).

So what is God's hang-up with idols? How could worshiping them be the worst of Judah's sins? I mean, really. They were doing some pretty horrible things. Selling their own family members into slavery to make themselves rich (Zech. 11:5) and "on your clothes is found the lifeblood of the innocent poor" (Jer. 2:34). With "the brazen look of a prostitute," they filled the land with adultery and prostitution, yet "refuse[d] to blush with shame" (3:3).

And in their case, everyone was doing it. God told Jeremiah, "If you can find but one person who deals honestly and seeks the truth, I will forgive this city" (5:1). But none could be found.

With so many other sins, how could worshiping idols be the worst?

As I searched this question out, the Scriptures overwhelmingly pointed to one thing.

Idols steal God's glory.

At the very core, the very essence of the issue, an inanimate, lifeless, created object steals the glory of the eternal Creator of life.

Yes, there were plenty of other atrocities the Israelites committed in connection with their idol worship, from male and female shrine prostitutes to sacrificing their own children to them. But above all, idols steal God's glory.

Before the dawn of the universe, the holy, all-wise, all-loving, all-powerful, infinite, just, merciful God chose to give us life and call us to Himself. From the beginning of creation to the sacrifice of His Son, God calls out for us to see His character and His worth. As the psalmist writes, "The heavens declare the glory of God; the skies proclaim the work of his hands. Day after day they pour forth speech; night after night they reveal knowledge" (19:1–2).

> **LIKE** an insidious illusionist,
> an idol misdirects our attention to itself.

But as God waits patiently to receive our awe, wonder, and appreciation for all He is and does, an idol steps in to accept our applause. Like an insidious illusionist, the idol misdirects our attention to itself. To better understand this theft of glory, consider that iconic idol, the golden calf (Exodus 32).

God had just revealed Himself to His chosen people Israel, who had cried out to Him under the terrible harsh treatment and bondage of slavery. In one of the greatest events in history, God didn't just set them free. He did it with style. Through ten plagues He humbled Egypt, the mightiest kingdom on earth, while simultaneously showing His power over all creation from life to death—from bringing a dead stick to life as a budding plant and carnivorous snake, to striking down the firstborn of those who chose not to acknowledge Him (Exodus 7–12).

Not only did the Lord set the Israelites free, but on the day of their release He made their Egyptian captors so favorably disposed to them that the Egyptians gave their freed slaves their riches as well, just as He predicted He would hundreds of years earlier (see Gen. 15:13–14; Ex. 12:41)! Later, when Pharaoh changed his mind and determined to reclaim his lost slaves, God put him and his mighty army to rest on the bottom of the Red Sea, while His people crossed over on dry land. The only Israelite to lift a hand in the skirmish was Moses raising his staff. Not one man, woman, or child was lost in the chase. God did all this to reveal His glory, to make His character and power known to the people He had chosen.

All this only scratched the surface of God's true glory. Just a peek to let the Israelites know how great their God truly was. When Moses asked God to show him His glory, God responded that no one could see His face and live. So God put him in the cleft of a rock, covered him with His hand, and passed by (Ex. 33:22).

Enter the golden calf. What does an idol do? Nothing. That's all an idol can do. Nothing. Nothing but steal God's glory.

THE master Money wants us to love it or fear it. Either one will do. Both would be better.

So while Moses was up on the Lord's holy mountain receiving the Law, given directly by God to His chosen leader so that he could govern the people justly, the people in their impatience crafted a golden calf out of the very riches God had just given them. And they appointed Aaron, the very person God had chosen as His high priest, to pronounce, "These are your gods, Israel, who brought you up out of Egypt" (Ex. 32:4).

That is why God despises idols.

God is a jealous God (Ex. 20:5). The prophet Malachi writes, "'A son honors his father, and a servant his master. If I am a father, where is the honor due me? If I am a master, where is the respect due me?' says the LORD Almighty. '. . . My name will be great among the nations, from where the sun rises to where it sets'" (1:6, 11).

Herein lies the heart of my second epiphany—a core truth to understanding Jesus' perspective on Money.

TRUTH:

Money, as an idol, steals God's glory.

Money's False Promises

Return to Jesus' words to His disciples and the large crowd He spoke to from the mountainside recorded by Matthew: "No one can serve two masters. Either you will hate the one and love the other, or you will be devoted to the one and despise the other. You cannot serve both God and money" (6:24).

Jesus clearly sets apart two competing masters.

On one hand, you have the true and living God. On the other hand, you have Money. Money characterized as a master.

Sometimes our *love* for God compels us to follow Him, to do the right thing, or not do the wrong thing, and other times our *fear* that He is a righteous Judge compels us.

It shouldn't surprise us, then, that the false master Money imitates the true master, God, by appealing to the same motivations. That is, Money wants us to love it or fear it. Either one will do. Both would be better.

In only a few words, Jesus cuts down all the motivators Money has at its disposal. However, in my slowness, it took me years to see this.

As a fake god, Money's only power is imitation. It falsely promises to give you the world. Even though the world isn't the idol's to give. The gifts Money gives are an illusion. Simply put, they aren't real.

AS a fake god, Money's only power is imitation. It falsely promises to give you the world. Even though the world isn't the idol's to give.

Enriched, Not Impoverished

In the children's movie *Flushed Away*, Roddy, the prized pet rat raised in a mansion, is flushed down his own potty, exposed to life as a sewer rat in the sewage flowing beneath the city. In the filth and sludge below, he is appalled to find the inhabitants of that world enmeshed in a battle over a sparkling piece of garbage held up to be the greatest of all jewels. He recognizes a fake when he sees one, because he was once surrounded by real jewels. But try as he might, he can't convince his new friends of the worthlessness of their prize.

We, as Christians, would benefit from Roddy's perspective. It is the perspective Jesus had. He'd come from his Father's side, and knew that there was no comparison between where He came from and where He was. Jesus is not trying to impoverish us when He tells us to store up treasures in heaven. He wants to enrich us. He's trying to get us to see that the good things we have here, as good as they are (and they are good—see Gen. 1:31), are dim reflections of the good things in the eternal life yet to come.

> **JESUS** is not trying to impoverish us when He tells us to store up treasures in heaven. He wants to enrich us.

But like Roddy's friends, we are slow to understand. I hear sermons about how few or how many treasures we might be allowed here on earth, and can't help but think how misplaced our hearts are when we think like that. If you have two piles of treasure, one that is real and one that is fake, do you really want to focus on what percentage of the fake stuff you get to keep?

It is obvious to all who live here that this world is under a curse. And it will come to an end. Everyone knows this, regardless of one's religion, philosophy, or creed. It's the age-old search for immortality, from Ponce de Leon's quest for the Fountain of Youth to the search for the Holy Grail to the Hindu belief in reincarnation. We see our mortality and want to avoid it. God has "set eternity in the human heart" (Eccl. 3:11). As a merciful loving God, He wants you to know that there is more. In heaven. He wants your heart there with Him.

God or Money: Who Will You Serve?

If you are at a point where Money does not have your heart, be warned that it still can master you. Through fear. The bondage is simple, the call is loud and strong.

"You need me."

"You can't live without me."

"Without me, you couldn't even buy lunch, let alone pay your rent. And how about when you get old?"

> JESUS means just what He says. You cannot love them both. You cannot fear them both. You must choose who you're going to serve. And who gets the glory.

Money scoffs, "Nice try, God, but welcome to the twenty-first century."

That's where Money had me. With fear.

A few moments earlier, Jesus had just said to give to everyone who asks, and this in the context of an evil person who wants to strike me, take my clothes, and sue me to boot! The old master Money was whacking me like a candy-crazy boy on a piñata, and mentally I was reeling.

In that fragile state of mind I finally realized exactly why Jesus followed up, "You cannot serve both God and money" with these words: "Therefore, I tell you, do not worry about your life, what you will eat or drink" (Matt. 6:25a). Not until we actually consider putting Jesus' words into practice do we begin to worry. Knowing this, Jesus follows up by saying,

> "So do not worry, saying, 'What shall we eat?' or 'What shall we drink?' or 'What shall we wear?' For the pagans run after all these things, and your heavenly Father knows that you need them. But seek first his kingdom and his righteousness, and all these things will be given to you as well." (Matt. 6:31–33)

Your Father has your back. Always has. Always will.

As I looked at God and Money in this new light, as competing masters vying for my heart, it became clear that Jesus means just what He says. You cannot love them both. You cannot fear them both. You must choose who you're going to serve. And who gets the glory.

4

For Richer or Poorer?

*"No one who has left home or brothers or
sisters or mother or father or children or fields
for me and the gospel will fail to receive a
hundred times as much in this present age."*

MARK 10:29–30

There is considerable debate in the church today as to whether God wants you rich or poor. Depending on the circle you run in—and I mean Christian circles—you'll likely run into a wide range of camps, from those who believe that God wants you rich, to those who believe that He wants you poor.

According to an article in *Time* magazine (2006), 61 percent of Christians surveyed believe that God wants people to be prosperous, 31 percent agreed that if you give your money to God, God will bless you with more money, and 17 percent consider themselves part of the Prosperity Theology movement (aka Health and Wealth, or Name It and Claim It). From this latter perspective, when it comes to wealth, "the new good news is that God doesn't want us to wait."[2] An opposing viewpoint is that worldly wealth is evidence that a person is greedy, self-centered, and unconcerned about the needs of others. What I call Poverty Is Piety Theology.

So which is it? Is wealth a blessing from God? Or a curse? Does Jesus want you rich? Or poor?

To answer this question, just about anyone familiar with anything Jesus ever said about rich people gravitates to Jesus' famous encounter with the rich young ruler in search of eternal life. Here is Mark's rendition of this encounter:

> As Jesus started on his way, a man ran up to him and fell on his knees before him. "Good teacher," he asked, "what must I do to inherit eternal life?"
>
> "Why do you call me good?" Jesus answered. "No one is good—except God alone. You know the commandments: 'You shall not murder, you shall not commit adultery, you shall not steal, you shall not give false testimony, you shall not defraud, honor your father and mother.'"

"Teacher," he declared, "all these I have kept since I was a boy."

Jesus looked at him and loved him. "One thing you lack," he said. "Go, sell everything you have and give to the poor, and you will have treasure in heaven. Then come, follow me."

At this the man's face fell. He went away sad, because he had great wealth.

Jesus looked around and said to his disciples, "How hard it is for the rich to enter the kingdom of God!"

The disciples were amazed at his words. But Jesus said again, "Children, how hard it is to enter the kingdom of God! It is easier for a camel to go through the eye of a needle than for someone who is rich to enter the kingdom of God."

The disciples were even more amazed, and said to each other, "Who then can be saved?"

Jesus looked at them and said, "With man this is impossible, but not with God; all things are possible with God."

Then Peter spoke up, "We have left everything to follow you!"

"Truly I tell you," Jesus replied, "no one who has left home or brothers or sisters or mother or father or children or fields for me and the gospel will fail to receive a hundred times as much in this present age: homes, brothers, sisters,

mothers, children and fields—along with persecutions—
and in the age to come eternal life. But many who are first
will be last, and the last first." (Mark 10:17–31)

Here, we find Jesus' mother of all metaphors related to rich
people. "It is easier for a camel to go through the eye of a needle
than for someone who is rich to enter the kingdom of God"
(Mark 10:25).

Bam! This is so huge that some argue it proves the Poverty Is Piety position. Q.E.D. *Quod erat demonstrandum*—that
"which was to be demonstrated"—the end of the philosophical
argument.

The Rationalizations

Suddenly, everyone living in a first-world country is nervous.
Does this metaphor relate to me? Jesus' statement appears so
strong and so unbending that otherwise rational people have
gone to incredible lengths to try to explain it away.

Like, "It doesn't relate to me. I'm not rich."

Or, "Jesus just told the rich dude to give away 'everything,'
because the guy didn't recognize he had a problem with money."

My personal favorite rationalization from biblical scholars
is the explanation that Jesus was referring to a narrow gate exit-
ing the city of Jerusalem called the "Eye of the Needle." As the
explanation goes, this extremely narrow gate gave travelers a
dickens of a time trying to get their large animals, especially

camels, through it. You had to unpack the camel, push, prod, and squeeze the beast through. A very difficult challenge, to be sure. But doable.

Whether this story is true or just a grandiose exercise in revisionist history, I have no idea. I simply cite it as proof of the lengths to which we are willing to go to explain away a passage that greatly troubles anyone with wealth who would like to inherit eternal life as well.

Certainly the passage is troubling to anyone who takes Jesus seriously. To anyone who doesn't try to explain away His words as just an exaggeration to make His point.

Jesus' disciples were certainly shocked. When He said of the rich young ruler, "How hard it is for a rich man to enter the kingdom of heaven," they were "greatly astonished" (Matt. 19:25) and "amazed" (Mark 10:24) at His words.

But have you ever stopped to wonder *why*? Why did His disciples respond this way? Jesus said many hard things in the presence of His disciples over the three years He spent with them. Many challenging things. Yet this is one of the very few times in the Bible when, by every account, His disciples were truly shocked. Why were they so taken aback by Jesus' words to this young man?

The answer has everything to do with the issue we are addressing here. The issue of whether God wants you rich or poor.

Why were they shocked?

Because they knew the Scriptures. As children in the

chosen tribe of Israel, they'd been weaned on God's Word. Not on the New Testament, which didn't yet exist, but rather on what we Christians call the Old Testament.

And the number one theme in all the Scriptures related to wealth is that it is a gift from God. I'll say it again. *Wealth is a gift from God.* Earthly possessions. Temporal treasures. Prosperity, abundance, riches.

If I argued before you today that money and wealth are not blessings, I would not only be guilty of reinterpreting the Scriptures to support my point, but I'd have the monumental task of explaining away the primary use of wealth in the Bible. Many years ago, when I searched for every passage of wealth in the Bible, well over 20 percent of the 1,300 passages I found fit into one category. *Treasures: Temporal.* Moreover, wealth in this category is almost singularly a blessing. Nowhere did I find a place where God promises to bless someone by impoverishing them.

WITH one deft metaphor, Jesus brought the Israelite version of the American Dream to an end.

This isn't to say that the poor aren't blessed. James points out that God has "chosen those who are poor in the eyes of the world to be rich in faith and to inherit the kingdom he promised those who love him" (2:5). However, poverty itself isn't the blessing. The kingdom is the blessing.

So when you see things from the disciples' perspective, you can see why they were astonished by Jesus' words, "It is easier for a camel to go through the eye of a needle than for someone who is rich to enter the kingdom of God" (Matt. 19:24). This rich, ruling young man was their poster boy for eternal life. And Jesus had just shot him down!

Think about it. If God blesses those who obey Him and curses those who do not—a very common and recurring theme in the Bible, even much more so in the Old Testament, the portion of Scripture available to people at that point in time—who could be a more deserving candidate for eternal life than this rich young ruler? Yet with one deft metaphor, Jesus brought the Israelite version of the American Dream to an end. He had dismissed the most meritorious candidate possible for eternal life.

Here is a young man who had obeyed God, who had kept the commandments since his youth, and who accordingly had been blessed by God, as promised in the Scriptures. I think the disciples expected Jesus to say, "Bingo! We have a winner! What do *you* need to do to inherit eternal life? Absolutely nothing! It's already yours. Welcome to the kingdom!"

But instead of saying this, Jesus said it is impossible for this rich young man, or any rich person, to enter the kingdom of heaven. It would be easier to stuff a seven-foot-tall, 2,200-pound hairy beast through a hole better suited for one of its hairs, than for this rich young man to enter the kingdom. And His disciples were greatly astounded. They were amazed.

All they could say was, "Who then can be saved?" (Mark 10:26).

The Great Omission

Here is where some people mistakenly make it about the money. They wrongly conclude that rich people can't make it to heaven, but poor people can. This is a grave error. In truth, no one can enter the kingdom of heaven, rich or poor, without God.

As proof, simply read Jesus' answer to his disciples' question, "Who then can be saved?" Jesus clearly answers, "With man it is impossible. But with God, all things are possible."

Anyone who still wants to use this encounter to argue that poverty equals piety has made an enormous omission. What I call the Great Omission.

They have omitted the rest of the story!

Because when Peter next states, "We have left everything to follow you!" Jesus replies, "Truly I tell you, no one who has left home or brothers or sisters or mother or father or children or fields for me and the gospel will fail to receive a *hundred times as much* in this present age . . ." (Mark 10:29–30, emphasis added). A hundred times as much!

This is not a promise or guarantee of increased material prosperity or improved financial status. But the truth is that those who leave everything to follow Jesus will be enriched (though, with persecutions [v. 30]) in this life *and* in the age to come. This "enriching" may take all kinds of forms through other believers, the church, and spiritual blessings as well.

Clearly the circumstances of Jesus' followers range from those who, like Peter, have given it all away, to those who have had multiplied back incredibly more—a person's godliness can hardly be measured by looking at their net worth.

The Good Thing

So, if the "rich young ruler" passage isn't about the money, what is the point of Jesus' encounter with him?

Return with me to the *beginning* of the story.

What did the young man come to Jesus looking for?

Eternal life.

"'Good teacher,' he asked, 'what must I do to inherit eternal life?'" (Mark 10:17).

At first blush, the quest for eternal life seems like a pretty noble search, a pretty *good* thing. Who doesn't want eternal life? This isn't just a Christian quest. This is humanity's quest. Every religion, every philosophy, every society must deal with the problem of death. And this young man who had everything the world could offer realized that it would all come to an end. He wanted eternal life.

IF we're seeking heaven because our life here is so good that we don't want it to end, or simply because we don't want to go to hell, we've missed the point. We've made the same mistake this young man made.

Jesus, however, wasn't going to waste the opportunity to let him know that his search was misguided. The young man was looking for the wrong "good" thing from the get-go.

We miss this, too, because we're looking for the same wrong thing. Eternal life.

We want to get to heaven. Great destination, especially when we've considered the alternative.

But if we're seeking heaven because our life here is so good that we don't want it to end, or simply because we don't want to go to hell, we've missed the point. We've made the same mistake this young man made.

So doing what Jesus always did, He redirected the young man to the right thing. The *greatest* good. He redirected the young man to God. Jesus clarifies that no one is *good* but God Himself.

Why? Because the young man, in his quest for eternal life, assumed that eternal life in and of itself was the good thing. And he was wrong.

Whereas Jesus knows the truth.

TRUTH:

Anything other than
God is the wrong "good" thing.

What makes eternal life good isn't the length. It's the company. *God Himself is what is good about heaven.* The gold streets, the many rooms, and the no departure date are all blessings, but they aren't the highlight. He is.

Living in God's presence is what makes heaven good. Peter got it right. "We have left everything to follow you!" Jesus explained this most succinctly as He prayed the night He was betrayed. "Now this is eternal life: that they know you, the only true God, and Jesus Christ, whom you have sent" (John 17:3).

WHAT makes eternal life good isn't the length. It's the company. *God Himself is what is good about heaven.* The gold streets, the many rooms, and the no departure date are all blessings, but they aren't the highlight. He is.

If you think I'm just mincing words, consider this: life in hell is equally long. But the company is considerably different. There, "the worms that eat them do not die, and the fire is not quenched" (Mark 9:48). Perhaps the real reason for "weeping and gnashing of teeth" (Matt. 13:42) is their eternal separation from the goodness of God. You see, we all get a chance to meet God at the judgment, where we will all see Him for who He is. And having done so, to be separated out as those who will spend eternity without Him will be sorrow upon sorrow. Weeping and gnashing of teeth.

But despite Jesus' question and follow-up statement, "Why do you call me good? No one is good—except God alone" (Mark 10:18), the young man misses it. He misses what is good. He is bent on getting what he came for. He wants eternal life.

I love how Mark captures Jesus' heart in this encounter: "Jesus looked at him and loved him" (Mark 10:21).

And so He tries again.

> **A RICH** person's wealth may numb their sense of their need for God, while a poor person's poverty may drive them to Him.

"You still lack one thing. Sell everything you have and give to the poor, and you will have treasure in heaven. Then come, follow me" (Luke 18:22).

Do you recall why Jesus said we should store up treasures in heaven? "For where your treasure is, there your heart will be also" (Matt. 6:21). God wants our hearts. Jesus' purpose remained single-minded throughout this encounter. "Then come, follow me" (Mark 10:21).

Again, choose what is supremely good—God—not the lesser thing.

But the young man didn't get it. He went away sad.

Why? Because he had a lot of the lesser blessing. He had "great wealth." He didn't understand that Jesus was offering so much more.

The Role of Money?

Finally, here is where this passage *is* about the money. A rich person's wealth may numb their sense of their need for God, while a poor person's poverty may drive them to Him. Regardless of how much of a blessing wealth has the potential to be, it becomes a curse for us when it separates us from the love of God.

Jesus cuts straight through our hypocrisy. He knows whether we have a heart for Him, or only for the good things that He has to offer. He sees our hearts clearly, even when we don't. What will you do when Jesus tests your heart? Will you go away sad, or respond like Job who, when all was stripped away, fell to the ground and worshiped. "Naked I came from my mother's womb, and naked I will depart. The LORD gave and the LORD has taken away; may the name of the LORD be praised" (Job 1:21).

Don't wrongfully conclude that rich people can't make it, but poor people can. Or that poor people are godly, but rich people are not. If we do this, we miss the point entirely. We think that Jesus is just calling out rich people. We think He is talking about people's financial position, when He's really talking about our heart condition.

So you see, it never was about the money per se. It was, is, and always will be about Him. Who do you love? And who do you fear?

At the end of the day, the answer to the question "Does Jesus want you rich or poor?" is obvious.

The answer is Yes!

Jesus wants you. Rich or poor.

And the answer is all about God's goodness, not ours.

5

The Great Deception

"Still others, like seed sown among thorns, hear the word; but the worries of this life, the deceitfulness of wealth and the desires for other things come in and choke the word, making it unfruitful."

MARK 4:18–19

Last chapter, I pointed out that the number one theme related to wealth in the Bible is that it is a blessing from God. Rational people have naturally concluded, then, that we should pursue it. What is wealth, after all? A tool! So why not get the biggest and best tool possible? Imagine the great things we could accomplish if money were no object.

Yet Jesus, in His parable of the sower, tells us that the "deceitfulness of wealth" chokes out the Word that He plants in us, making our lives unfruitful (Matt. 13:22). His warnings against wealth's deceitfulness highlight the second-most common category related to wealth in the Bible: what I've titled, "*Deceitfulness related to wealth; greed*." Though everything we have is from God, somehow wealth has the potential to become a curse for us.

But if wealth is a blessing, how does this happen?

Quite simply, we are deceived.

The Two Faces of Deception

Years ago, our pastor, Dave Bechtel, made a list of all the things God promises us in the Scriptures. I don't remember all the details, but it was quite a heady list. He had a whole column filled with things like:

GOD'S PROMISES

1. Meet all your needs (Philippians 4:19)
2. Full/abundant life (John 10:10)
3. Peace (John 14:27)
4. Security/shield (Psalm 3:3)
5. Fortress/rock (Psalm 18:2)
6. Hope (Psalm 71:5)
7. Help (Psalm 121:1–2; Hebrews 13:6)
8. Lifts me up (Psalm 3:3)

MONEY'S PROMISES

1. _____
2. _____
3. _____
4. _____
5. _____
6. _____
7. _____
8. _____

9. Healer (Psalm 147:3)	9. _____
10. Provider (Psalm 23:1)	10. _____
11. A future (Jeremiah 29:11)	11. _____
12. Rest (Matthew 11:28–29)	12. _____
13. Strength/power (Isaiah 40:29)	13. _____

And so on.

Next to it he had a list of Money's promises, covered up on the screen.

When he unveiled Money's promises, to all our surprise, it was the same list!

I suppose it shouldn't have surprised us, had we just taken the time to think about it. James, the brother of Jesus, explains, "*Don't be deceived*, my dear brothers and sisters. Every good and perfect gift is from above, coming down from the Father of the heavenly lights, who does not change like shifting shadows" (James 1:16–17, emphasis added). Since everything good comes from God, all that is left for the fake master to offer is imitation. So Money offers the same promises as God. But with the added bonus that you make the call. You decide what's good for you. You don't have to wait on the Lord.

"Get what you want!"

"Get what you need!"

"Get what you deserve!"

"Now!"

I'd even argue that, from the world's perspective, Money

offers you *more* than God does. Because there are certain things you can buy that God just won't give you. Like a mistress. Or revenge. Or anything else that goes against who He is. Things that aren't kind, just, or right.

Let me be clear that there is a huge difference between *offering more* and *delivering more*. Much like what Satan offered when he tried to tempt Jesus. "'All this I will give you,' he said, 'if you will bow down and worship me'" (Matt. 4:9). In truth, it wasn't his to give. But he offered it just the same.

So James warns, "Don't be deceived."

But deception has a second, more familiar face. Our own. We can also *deceive ourselves*. James warns, "Do not merely listen to the word, and so *deceive yourselves*. Do what it says" (James 1:22, emphasis added).

The Deception of Eve

In case you missed it, the very first sin in human history involved deception. And I'm not talking about the serpent. Yes, Satan has been sinning since the beginning. He is the father of lies. But I'm talking about Eve. The one who was deceived.

If you're like me, you must have wondered how our ancestors could have messed up a situation as cool as the garden of Eden. When we look back to the garden, it seems almost unimaginable that Adam and Eve would do the one thing God commanded them not to do. Seriously! Think about it. They took evening walks with God. Plus, they had each other. And they ruled over paradise. What, then, could be so desirable that they would give all that up? Here's how the deception went down:

> Now the serpent was more crafty than any of the wild animals the LORD God had made. He said to the woman, "Did God really say, 'You must not eat from any tree in the garden'?"
>
> The woman said to the serpent, "We may eat fruit from the trees in the garden, but God did say, 'You must not eat fruit from the tree that is in the middle of the garden, and you must not touch it, or you will die.'"
>
> "You will not certainly die," the serpent said to the woman. "For God knows that when you eat from it your eyes will be opened, and you will be like God, knowing good and evil."
>
> When the woman saw that the fruit of the tree was good for food and pleasing to the eye, and also desirable for gaining wisdom, she took some and ate it. (Gen. 3:1–6)

Notice it all started with a question. "Did God really say . . . ?" (Gen. 3:1b). In fact, it is the very first question recorded in the Bible. Too bad Eve hadn't taken my first sales class, and learned the rule, "He who asks the questions controls the conversation." Or knew what professors know—that with some questions, even the right answer just sounds wrong. Like, "Have you stopped beating your wife?" Either way, you lose. But alas, the world was new, and Eve naïve.

THE serpent knew he had Eve on thin ice. Because there was only one way for Eve to support her answer. She had to trust God, 100 percent.

So the serpent asked a question that appeared to be about the rules: "Did God really say . . . ?" But he wasn't really asking a question about the rules at all. He didn't want to know which tree was which. Rather, he was questioning God's character. Could God be trusted?

When Eve answered with facts about the trees, the serpent switched his attack to a direct challenge to God's integrity. To God's trustworthiness. He said to her, "You will not certainly die" (Gen. 3:4).

The serpent knew he had Eve on thin ice. Because there was only one way for Eve to support her answer. She had to trust God, 100 percent. What other evidence did she have? She couldn't point to any examples as proof that she would die. No one had ever died before! Her answer required complete faith in God.

The serpent saw the opening and took it, challenging God's motive for withholding the fruit. "God knows . . . you will be like God" (Gen. 3:5).

In essence, the serpent implied God had a motive to deceive her. That God wanted to keep Himself above her. Could she really trust Him?

With Eve's head now spinning, the serpent made the offer of a lifetime. Eve could "be like God, knowing good and evil" (Gen. 3:5b).

Talk about the mother of all carrots. "Be like God." And get smart along the way!

What was Eve's desire? To be like God. What could be better than that? No offense to Adam. Great guy, I'm sure. But compared to God, Adam couldn't have looked like much.

The serpent pointed out to Eve that she had a deficiency. That unlike God, she didn't know the difference between good and evil. If only . . .

So the serpent planted a seed of mistrust.

Was the serpent right? Could she really be as amazing as God, if only she ate of the forbidden fruit? If only she obtained the knowledge of good and evil?

EVE chose to trust in the serpent,
and she chose to trust in herself. And in
doing so, she was deceived by both.

Like all deceptions, the serpent started with a grain of truth. The truth is that God does know good and evil. But not as the serpent suggested. God knows evil by observing it, not by participating in it. By *doing* evil, Eve also knew the difference between the two. But not as God knows them. In the end, she not only didn't become like God, she was separated from Him.

Eve chose to trust in the serpent, and she chose to trust in herself. And in doing so, she was deceived by both. Yes, the serpent misled her. But she also deceived herself. She trusted in her *senses* (the "fruit of the tree was good for food and pleasing to the eye"), and she trusted in her intellect, or *reason* ("and also desirable for gaining wisdom").

Like Eve, we can *be deceived* by another, or we can *deceive ourselves*. Either way, we miss the good God has planned for our lives. Both lead down the same road, and end in death.

The Heart of Deception

At the heart of every deception lies a key principle. What I call the Great Deception: *our belief that we have a better plan for our lives than God does.*

We are deceived whenever we think that we have a better plan for our lives than God does.

Whenever we conclude that the plans we have for our lives are better than the plans He has for us, or that the gifts we have for ourselves are better than His gifts, the false master Money steps up. Money promises to put us in charge. With it, we can smooth the way or save the day. Don't worry. Be happy.

But God has a better plan for our lives. We were made to live for so much more. And *He* is more. God wants us to understand and know Him, His "kindness, justice and righteousness," for in these He delights (Jer. 9:24). God's plan is to complete us.

So Jesus tells a parable about a farmer, His Father, who sows some seed—His Word, the message about the kingdom of God. The seed has the potential to yield an enormous return, up to a hundred times what it was. Yet many circumstances interfere, causing some of the seed to be wasted. Worthless. And wealth is one of those circumstances.

WITH wealth come weeds. Weeds that can choke out the very life He desires.

Seed that falls on rich soil grows rapidly, but so do the weeds, so that when it comes time to harvest the crop, the farmer gets nothing of value. All plant, no produce. Likewise, riches increase the risk we won't mature. We look good, but come to nothing. With wealth come weeds. Weeds that can choke out the very life He desires. In such an end, we are left with nothing. No wonder Paul warns,

> Those who want to get rich fall into temptation and a trap and into many foolish and harmful desires that plunge people into ruin and destruction. For the love of money is a root of all kinds of evil. Some people, eager for money, have wandered from the faith and pierced themselves with many griefs. (1 Tim. 6:9–10)

Indeed, a quick skim of the Scriptures reveals examples where every one of the Ten Commandments are broken in various quests for wealth.

Unmasking Deception

One reason that we are so easily deceived is that we are often mistaken about what makes something good or bad. We make a list of the bad things in this world and try with all our might to avoid them. Or we make a list of good things and try to get more of them. We mistakenly think things like sex, drugs, wealth, or power are bad, in and of themselves, or that peace and knowledge are good, in and of themselves. The truth is, "He has made everything beautiful in its time" (Eccl. 3:11).

Take drugs, for example. A couple years back, I had knee surgery. And I watched the whole thing in living color on the monitor above my head. Me—a guy who would rather be shot than get a shot. When it was over, I looked up at my iodine-soaked leg, elevated straight up over me between two nurses who were sponging it off. Were it not for the telltale signs of the foot fungus I'd been trying to eradicate for years, I wouldn't have even known that it was mine. I could feel my leg lying on the table next to my other one. So what was it doing up there in the air? I was so numb to the pain, they could have walked right out of the hospital with my leg, and I'd have never known.

Such is the beauty of drugs. In their proper time and place.

Similarly, wealth, like all of creation, is a wonderful gift from God—when humbly submitted to His lordship. Search the Scriptures and you will frequently find God promise to bless with prosperity those who follow Him. Yet you would be hard-pressed to find a place where He says that He will curse someone with wealth. Instead, wealth becomes a curse for us when we choose it over Him.

We're quick to point the finger at someone else when we turn His blessings into curses. Eve blamed the serpent. Adam blamed Eve. And in a backhanded way, he even blamed God, claiming his downfall was caused by "the woman you put here with me" (Gen. 3:12). No wonder our sins separate us from God. He gives us something good, and we choose it over Him. Then, when it all goes wrong, we discredit Him or His gift. In our effort to absolve ourselves from guilt, we exchange the glory due Him for a lie.

But James explains, "When tempted, no one should say, 'God is tempting me.' For God cannot be tempted by evil, nor does he tempt anyone" (1:13).

Why can't God be tempted by evil? Because everything God created is good. All of creation is a wonderful gift from God—when humbly submitted to His lordship. In its proper place and time.

God doesn't create amazing things to tempt us. He creates amazing things because He is an amazing Creator. Would we rather Him give us grey flowers? Food without flavor? Air without aroma?

Acknowledging that God's good gifts are exactly that—good gifts—James goes on to give what I've found to be the clearest description of deception's path in the entire Bible. "Each person is tempted when they are dragged away by their own *evil desire* and enticed. Then, after desire has conceived, it *gives birth to sin*; and sin, when it is full-grown, *gives birth to death*" (James 1:14–15, emphasis added).

Here, then, is the path: *evil desire* gives birth to *sin*, which in turn gives birth to *death.*

What Makes Evil Desire Evil?

In its simplest form, *evil desire becomes evil when we desire something for ourselves that is outside of God's plan for us.* But defining evil desire this way, I freely admit that I am in danger of reducing evil desire to what philosophers call a *tautology*: that which is true by definition. This is distasteful to philosophers, who argue that we should use reason to determine right from wrong. The problem with reason, however, is that once you add self-interest, you can rationalize almost anything. Benjamin Franklin once wrote, "So convenient a thing it is to be a reasonable creature, since it enables one to find or make a reason for everything one has a mind to do."[3]

So while I would agree that the things of God are confirmed by reason, they are still true regardless. Regardless of whether I understand His reasoning or not.

As Christians, we have a decided advantage to guide our

reasoning. God has directly given us His Word. But it only protects us from deception if we do what He says.

To eliminate evil desires, some have proposed to eradicate pleasure altogether. It is astounding how many philosophies are centered on the idea of pleasure. Hedonists think that the whole of life is about obtaining it. Utilitarians strive to maximize pleasure and minimize pain. At the other extreme, ascetics try to break the bond of worldly pleasure by avoiding it altogether. Many religions, including sects of Hinduism, Buddhism, and even some forms of Christianity, take a similar view.

To be sure, there are corrupt pleasures that are not from God (Prov. 18:2; Heb. 11:25; Titus 3:3). Such pleasures can master us. Or be used by another to do so. Peter warns of those who would enslave us to benefit themselves, "for 'people are slaves to whatever has mastered them'" (2 Peter 2:19).

But we need to understand that pleasure itself is not the issue, just as the things we associate with pleasure are not. The psalmist speaks of eternity, saying, "You will fill me with joy in your presence, with eternal pleasures at your right hand" (Ps. 16:11). If pleasure itself is bad, then someone could rightly say, "God is tempting me." Because God makes amazing things. Things that are pleasing.

Like Eve. Those who hope to kill desire would never have invented her. Adam needed a helper in the garden, right? Utilitarians would have given him a shovel. What could be more helpful in a garden than that? But God, in His infinite wisdom, gives gifts beyond all that we imagine. Adam might have thanked God for a shovel. Politely. But of Eve, he said, "Wow! Now that's what I'm talking about!" Or something to that effect. God's ways are infinitely above ours.

And so it is not any of God's gifts that make our desires evil. Rather, *desire becomes evil when we desire something for ourselves outside of His plan.*

God is not tempted by evil, because to do so, He would have to be untrue to Himself. He would have to act contrary to His character—to His kindness, justice, and righteousness. But He is the giver of "every good and perfect gift" (James 1:17). For His glory. God sees the path, from start to finish. He can see the end from the beginning, and He knows those paths that end in death.

When we choose to trust anyone, even ourselves, in place of God, we are deceived.

Are you deceived? Take the simple test below to find out.

PART 1:

If money were no object, what would you buy?

Don't rush through this. Make a list. Make it as long as you want. And think big. Beauty-pageant big. Like "world peace." Or a better education. Or a spouse. Also, think small. Like straight white teeth, or an A on a test.

I've provided a whole page, so go ahead, make your list. And take your time. This is important.

MY LIST

1.
2.
3.
4.
5.
6.
7.
8.
9.
10.
11.
12.
13.
14.
15.
16.
17.
18.
19.
20.

What did you come up with? A better neighborhood? Better schools? Better opportunities? Abs of steel? Security for your children? Better education, healthcare, retirement? Peace? Nice hair? Any hair? Money to give to a friend in need? Money to support God's work in the world?

PART 2:
Put a checkmark next to the things on your list that you think God will never give you.

These are the areas where you are most vulnerable to being deceived and mastered by Money. Every program I've ever heard of to get over an addiction, or a sin, begins with recognizing you have a problem. Look back over the list of things you would buy if you had enough money, and pay special attention to those with checkmarks—those things that you don't think God will give you. Regardless of how good they might be in and of themselves, recognize that this is where Money has the power to master you. I encourage you to pray over this list, and ask God to protect you. And if necessary, to set you free.

6

Just Money

"For whoever has will be given more, and they will have an abundance. Whoever does not have, even what they have will be taken from them."

MATTHEW 25:29

There is a longstanding battle between the "haves" and the "have nots." And regardless of who you are, you can't help but have an opinion on the subject. Pope Francis, the most popular pope in recent memory, has taken a stand against income inequality, and the watching world is fascinated as he shuns the papal mansion for the guest cottage, chooses to drive himself rather than be chauffeured about in a limousine, and expressed openness to crashing on someone's floor during his tour of the United States.[4] Major political movements like

Occupy Wall Street rail against the "one percent," that small fraction of wealthy citizens who presumably got that way through others' pain or unfair advantage.

How, then, can Jesus tell a parable where one man starts with five times as much as another, ends with ten times as much, and conclude that this is the good guy (Matt. 25:14–30)? To make matters worse, he tells his servants to take the little the poor servant has, give it to the rich one, and throw the wicked, lazy servant outside. "For whoever has will be given more, and they will have an abundance. Whoever does not have, even what they have will be taken from them" (Matt. 25:29).

If this seems patently unfair to you, you're not alone. In the parallel version of this parable in Luke, the other servants protest, exclaiming, "Sir, he already has ten!" (19:25).

What was Jesus thinking? His parable sounds like Robin Hood in reverse. Take from the poor and give to the rich. Where is the justice in that?

Not surprisingly, both wealth and justice are huge topics in the Bible. We think about these things from the womb. People say that a baby's first word is "mom," but my sons' first word was "mine." Yes, Alyssa claims it was "mom," but I think she misunderstood. Babies have trouble enunciating clearly.

Closely after their first word came their first rhetorical statement. "That's not fair." As a young father, I had a hard time with this—being lectured by a two-year-old on fairness. What could my son possibly know about justice? He's only two! But a two-year-old is smart enough to figure out that his four-year-old brother got two crackers when he only got one. And so it begins. The quest for *equality*.

The four-year-old has a more developed sense of justice. He thinks he *deserves* two crackers, because they were a reward for picking up the toys, and his little brother didn't pick up any. In fact, he thinks he was shorted by only getting two crackers to his brother's one. He thinks he deserves all three. He demands *equity*.

> **WE** accuse those who judge us of "playing God," but we aren't so happy about God playing Himself, either. And His judgments are right.

Most justice and fairness arguments are based on these two concepts: equality and equity. *Equality* is treating everyone the same, without regard to merit. *Equity*, on the other hand, metes out justice based on merit. Basing justice or fairness on equity is more complicated than when it is based on equality, because equity requires more judgment. Equality looks only to the equal size of the reward or punishment, whereas equity requires an additional judgment on the action performed to merit the reward or punishment.

Probably the most recited verse in the whole Bible is "Do not judge" (Matt. 7:1; Luke 6:37). Even atheists tout this one. People hate to be judged. We often blame this on wrong judgments by our fellow man, but this is only part of it. We accuse those who judge us of "playing God," but we aren't so happy about God playing Himself, either. And His judgments are right.

Wisdom, Wealth, and Justice

To be sure, Jesus challenges our understanding of the poor. If you were to ask ten people the question, "Where do poor people come from?" you'd probably get ten different answers, all based on people's observations and experiences. There seem to be so many factors. Birth, fortune and misfortune, justice and injustice, blessings and curses, good choices and bad. And while undoubtedly you'd get some themes in common, quite likely they'd miss the obvious answer.

Poor people come from God. Exactly the same place as rich people.

Having acknowledged the obvious, I return to the important question, "Why are some people poor and others rich?"

The answer to this question has everything to do with Jesus' parable of the talents (Matt. 25:14–30). In this parable,

Jesus refers to three servants, each receiving a different amount of money to manage, based on their ability. In doing so, Jesus acknowledges that not everyone is the same. Some are simply more gifted than others. Note that all three are working for the same master. This is important, because your boss, location, economic and political systems, war and peace, and historic time periods are all factors that could impact our money management. But since these are the same for all three servants, when the master returns and calls his servants to account, no one had an unfair advantage. The ones who did well with a few things were put in charge of many things. But the one who gave way to fear and buried what was entrusted to him was thrown "outside, into the darkness, where there will be weeping and gnashing of teeth" (Matt. 25:30).

Set aside for a moment that these last words are a metaphor for hell.

The justice in Jesus' judgment is extremely important for us to understand. In calling out this servant as "lazy" and "wicked" (Matt. 25:26), Jesus calls attention to the two biggest factors relating wisdom to wealth in the entire book of Proverbs. It is expressly designed "for receiving instruction in prudent behavior, doing what is right and just and fair" (1:3). And Proverbs, the heart of what biblical scholars call the Wisdom Literature, discusses money and worldly wealth more than any other book in the Bible.

Diligence over Sloth

The number one theme in Proverbs relating wisdom to wealth is *diligence over sloth*. Do something and you'll have something. Don't and you won't.

When I was five, my parents bought the farm. Literally, not figuratively. Twenty acres Northeast of Portland, in Vancouver, Washington, with the most beautiful views of Mount St. Helens and Mount Hood you can imagine. We kids thought they were crazy. Instead of a cute little house in the suburbs, for the same price we got two houses, one functioning electrical outlet, a chicken coop, and an old barn. Dad was a forester and Mom stayed home with the four kids, ages five to nine.

When we moved in, my siblings and I were pretty sure the houses were haunted, especially the one next door, where Mrs. Curtin had died. We didn't know much about the old lady, but she was the last of the clan. We'd found a broken-off old tombstone with Curtin carved in it and figured her husband was probably buried somewhere on the farm. One night when our cousins visited, figuring safety in number, we took flashlights over to explore. Going up the narrow stairs to the attic, a loud thumping passed us. I never saw Mrs. Curtin's head bounce by, but Joe said it did, and his word was good enough for me. I didn't return for my shorts.

It's been forty-five years since my parents converted the place into a Christmas tree farm. The houses are painted, the barn's been reroofed, and they've expanded to fifty acres, compliments of Dad's business model—"An overly ambitious father with not-too-bright sons." Thousands of families come from Portland and Vancouver to Thorntons' Treeland for the free hayrides and petting zoo, free coffee and hot chocolate, and for the memories. And hopefully they buy a tree. The "not-too-bright sons" have been replaced by "not-too-bright grandsons," who wouldn't know how good they've got it if their dads didn't tell them.

Meanwhile, the neighbors' land is covered with brush. At one time it was fenced for cattle, though you'd never know it now. When we were kids, exploring or looking for a lost steer, we'd discovered the remains of old fences, but even then they were covered with blackberry vines. They've never taken any crops off their land. Never raised any cattle. A quarter mile up the street, our closest neighbor besides the Curtin house, was a big two-story Craftsman home built in the early 1900s. I loved that house. Big gables. Bay window. Somebody rented it out. A hole in the roof grew so big that they covered it with a tarp, which worked for a couple of years, but the Northwest gets too much rain, and the tarp didn't hold. A couple years back, somebody finally tore the house down. The big red barn beside it collapsed.

What I witnessed unfold over four decades is not a new phenomenon. Three thousand years ago Solomon described a similar scene:

I went past the field of the sluggard, past the vineyard of the man who has no sense; thorns had come up everywhere, the ground was covered with weeds, and the stone wall was in ruins. I applied my heart to what I observed and learned a lesson from what I saw: A little sleep, a little slumber, a little folding of the hands to rest—and poverty will come on you like a thief and scarcity like an armed man. (Prov. 24:30–34)

So do something.

Righteousness over Wickedness

The second-most common theme relating wisdom to wealth is *righteousness over wickedness*.

Stories of deception, fraud, and exploitation fill the news, no matter where you are. I spent New Year's Eve in Lincoln City, a small coastal town in Oregon, and every one of the top ten stories of the year was either financial fraud or a sex scandal. No wonder people think you have to cheat to get ahead. The logic is pretty straightforward. We live in a fallen world. To get ahead in an unjust world, you've got to be that way yourself. It is easy for us to conclude that the path to wealth is through unjust means.

But God doesn't see it that way. Rather, it is the righteous who prosper. Contrary to what some might think, wisdom tells us, "With me are riches and honor, enduring wealth and prosperity. . . . I walk in the way of righteousness, along the paths of justice, bestowing a rich inheritance on those who love me and making their treasures full" (Prov. 8:18, 20–21). And despite the transitory nature of earthly wealth, the wages of the righteous tend to persist. Even for generations. Not so the wicked. "A good person leaves an inheritance for their children's children, but a sinner's wealth is stored up for the righteous" (Prov. 13:22).

The opposite of righteousness is wickedness. The wicked acquire wealth through dishonest scales (Prov. 11:1; 20:10), deceptive wages (11:18), hoarding (11:26), greed, fraud, and oppression (22:16). And while the wealth of the wicked often soars to great heights, its glory is brief, and the end is certain, whether in this life or the one to come.

The Proverbs explain that dishonest money is illusory. It dwindles away (13:11), is of no value (10:2), brings the wicked punishment (10:16), and is worthless in the day of wrath (11:4). Why? Because the wicked "lie in wait for their own blood" (1:18). "Such are the paths of all who go after ill-gotten gain; it takes away the life of those who get it" (1:19).

So do not envy the arrogant when you see the prosperity of the wicked, as Asaph almost did (Psalm 73). Rather, understand their final destiny. God has placed "them on slippery ground. . . . How suddenly are they destroyed, completely swept away by terrors" (73:18–19). For "though the righteous fall seven times, they rise again, but the wicked stumble when calamity strikes" (Prov. 24:16).

So what is the takeaway?

Do something. And do it right. Honestly, diligently, without oppression, exploitation, hoarding, fraud, or greed.

No wonder Jesus called out the servant for being wicked and lazy. And He calls us out as well. Undoubtedly there will be times when we face injustice in this fallen world, when we are mistreated, cheated, or oppressed (Prov. 13:23). But we must be careful not to hide behind the injustices of others to mask our own laziness or wickedness.

We serve a God who judges the thoughts and intents of the heart. So don't be discouraged when you face trials of many kinds. Even Job, commended by God as the most blameless and upright man on earth (Job 1:8), experienced not only material blessing but unfathomable loss. "In all this, Job did not sin by charging God with wrongdoing" (1:22). In the same way, God calls us to do what is right, and leave the justice to Him.

Generosity over Stinginess

There is a third category in Proverbs tying wealth to wisdom that we must not overlook. And it is as important as it is counterintuitive. "One person gives freely, yet gains even more; another withholds unduly, but comes to poverty" (Prov. 11:24). Somehow, in the Proverbs, the one who is generous gets more, and the one who withholds gets less.

You must be asking, "How can this be?" Is this new math?

I'm no genius, but I can tell you with the confidence of a seasoned accountant that if you have ten dollars and give three away, you only have seven left. You don't have more. You have less.

How can the Bible say otherwise?

Here are two explanations, both of which I think are true.

First, generosity leads to more because God is sovereign. And in His sovereignty, He rewards those who obey him in faith by doing the work He has called us to. Solomon put it this way: "Whoever is kind to the poor lends to the LORD, and he will reward them for what they have done" (Prov. 19:17). In our limited wisdom, we mistakenly "do the math" using what economists call a "zero-sum game." If one person has, the other doesn't. But God, Creator of all things and true owner of all that exists, can say, "Go ahead. Give it away. I'll make more."

> WE hold on to everything we have so we can get even more, but in our greed and stinginess, we come to poverty.

Second, generosity leads to more because it changes us. This is something I've noticed in my own attitude, and you've probably noticed in yours.

When our thoughts revolve around being generous, our eyes are open to those who have less than we do. We're looking for the opportunity to give, and in doing so we realize how blessed we truly are. We see all those in need, and are thankful that God has so blessed us that we have something to give. And we are *content*. The apostle Paul affirmed, "Godliness with contentment is great gain" (1 Tim. 6:6).

The opposite is true when we are stingy. In our stinginess, we see the things other people have that we don't, and we covet them. We are jealous and ungrateful. Note that even the richest person in the world still does not own most of it. And so we are discontent, and we must have more. We hold on to everything we have so we can get even more, but in our greed and stinginess, we come to poverty.

Paul warns Timothy, "Those who want to get rich fall into temptation and a trap and into many foolish and harmful desires that plunge people into ruin and destruction" (1 Tim. 6:9).

Made for More

From the very first blessing in the Bible, "Be fruitful and increase" (Gen. 1:22), to the very first psalm, "whatever they do prospers" (Ps. 1:3), a life well-lived bears fruit. Acknowledging that prosperity is a blessing—that having food, clothing, and a warm, dry place to live is more preferable than being hungry, naked, and homeless, that having something to share and provide for others is preferable to having overspent, begging for bread or leniency from the bank—it is fitting to see what God says about obtaining it.

Despite the curse we are now under, the principle remains the same.

TRUTH:

There is a wisdom-wealth connection: do something, do it right, and be generous.

We must understand the God-ordained connection between wisdom and wealth for two reasons. The first is to acknowledge that God's ways work. If putting wisdom into practice results in blessings here, how much more will we be blessed eternally. What He created is good, and foreshadows even better things to come.

Second, we need to understand that despite the prosperity and wealth associated with wisdom, it is wisdom rather than wealth that is to be desired. From the city gates, wisdom cries out, "Choose my instruction instead of silver, knowledge rather than choice gold, for wisdom is more precious than rubies, and nothing you desire can compare with her" (Prov. 8:10–11).

DESPITE the prosperity and wealth
associated with wisdom, it is wisdom
rather than wealth that is to be desired.

The Lesser Blessing

Other things being equal, wealth is a blessing. But other things
are not always equal. For example, "Better a little with the fear
of the LORD than great wealth with turmoil" (Prov. 15:16). And,
"Better a small serving of vegetables with love than a fattened
calf with hatred" (15:17). More is less when it accompanies injustice (16:8), lies (19:22), oppression, and arrogance (16:19).
So while worldly wealth may be a blessing, it is the lesser
blessing.

Solomon summarizes, "The beginning of wisdom is this:
Get wisdom. Though it cost all you have, get understanding"
(Prov. 4:7). He sheds some light on why the former is better
than the latter: "For the protection of wisdom is like the protection of money, and the advantage of knowledge is that wisdom
preserves the life of him who has it" (Eccl. 7:12 ESV).

I recently led a group of students through Europe, a continent littered with the remains of despots and dictators who for 2,500 years ignored the proverb's warning, "The wealth of the rich is their fortified city; they imagine it a wall too high to scale" (Prov. 18:11), apparently unaware that "wealth is worthless in the day of wrath" (11:4) and that those "who trust in their riches will fall" (11:28).

At the end of the day, the fear of the Lord is the beginning of wisdom (Prov. 9:10), and wisdom put into practice through diligence, righteousness, and generosity frequently results in worldly wealth. But worldly wealth is the lesser blessing. Unlike wisdom, it cannot extend your life. Unlike righteousness, it doesn't protect you in the day of wrath. And if it comes at the expense of others, or a good name, or peace, it simply isn't worth much. It's just money.

A Proper Fool

"You fool! This very night your life will be demanded from you. Then who will get what you have prepared for yourself?"

LUKE 12:20

Do something. Do it right. And be generous. Wisdom's three simple rules that generally lead to prosperity. As a rule, becoming a millionaire isn't luck. It is learned. The classic book *The Millionaire Next Door* busted the myth that most millionaires in America were born with it. In fact, 80 percent of millionaires in the United States are first-generation rich.[5] They earned it. They did something, and did it right. Just like the Proverbs say. Welcome to the American Dream!

It all makes perfect sense. Until you listen to Jesus.

And he told them this parable: "The ground of a certain rich man yielded an abundant harvest. He thought to himself, 'What shall I do? I have no place to store my crops.'

"Then he said, 'This is what I'll do. I will tear down my barns and build bigger ones, and there I will store my surplus grain. And I'll say to myself, "You have plenty of grain laid up for many years. Take life easy; eat, drink and be merry."'

"But God said to him, 'You fool! This very night your life will be demanded from you. Then who will get what you have prepared for yourself?'

"This is how it will be with whoever stores up things for themselves but is not rich toward God."
(Luke 12:16–21)

And in so few words, Jesus crushes the American Dream.

Just to recap, this man *did something*. He earned his crop. And he *did it right*. There is no mention of cheating, theft, or dishonesty. Then he *saved* what he earned, and *retired* with plans to *enjoy* his remaining years.

How, then, is this man a fool?

If he is a fool, he is certainly a different kind of fool than the one identified by Solomon. This fool is downright reputable. For every Christian with a financial planner or a financial plan, Jesus' condemnation of this man is a stark contradiction to responsible living.

This man's life is so consistent with what we teach about financial planning in business school and in the church today that we are flooded with a myriad of troubling questions. What is Jesus saying?

Is it wrong to *save*?

Is it wrong to *retire*?

Is it wrong to *enjoy* what you earn?

If these are things you have been working for, you can't help but ask, "Why is this man the fool?"

In calling this man a fool, Jesus reveals one of the most overlooked truths about money in all the Scriptures. And missing this truth has not only destroyed many prosperous Christians, but emptied the church of its impact throughout history.

TRUTH:

God made us for more. More than ourselves, and more than this world.

The rich fool certainly missed this. He thought God made him rich so he could spend the rest of his life doing nothing. Or anything else he wanted. But God prospers us so that we can be rich toward Him. "From everyone who has been given much, much will be demanded" (Luke 12:48).

What will you do if God makes you prosper?

I cannot overstate the importance of your answer to this question. Because prosperity comes with tremendous responsibility. Job understood this (Job 31:13–28), answering his accusers, "If I have seen anyone perishing for lack of clothing, or the needy without garments, and their hearts did not bless me for warming them with the fleece from my sheep" (vv. 19–20), then he would dread destruction from God. Daniel understood it, faithfully serving his captors so well that in the end, God's name was exalted in the kingdoms of Babylon and Persia (Daniel 4 and 6). And Joseph understood it, forgiving his brothers who sold him into slavery, by saying, "You intended to harm me, but God intended it for good to accomplish what is now being done, the saving of many lives" (Gen. 50:20).

Those who do not understand this truth should hear, and fear, the words the prophet Ezekiel spoke to God's chosen people, "Now this was the sin of your sister Sodom: She and her daughters were arrogant, overfed and unconcerned; they did not help the poor and needy" (16:49).

Like the rich fool, it is easy to get "more" wrong. Because His blessings aren't for us alone. While God made us for more, worldly wealth isn't it. Worldly wealth is the lesser blessing. We are to be "rich toward God."

Treasures in Heaven

Sometime back, a wild-eyed young man named Josiah stormed into my office in a great state of agitation. A theology prof had spoken in chapel that morning and told him rich people were evil. It was the poor who were blessed. I'd spoken in chapel a few months earlier, and Josiah apparently preferred what I had to say. That you couldn't judge a person by their net worth. Josiah wanted a Ferrari. He wanted to retire a millionaire. At age thirty. He wanted it all.

I told him I appreciated his enthusiasm, that I sensed he had a strong work ethic, but that he'd been duped. He was settling for the lesser blessing. Why not go for treasures in heaven? That's what Jesus told us to do (Matt. 6:19–20).

Sullen, he grumbled, "What would I do with a crown?" He had no idea what treasures in heaven are. And so he couldn't imagine wanting them. Like Josiah, many of us find it hard to pursue treasures in heaven, because we don't really know what they are. Instead, we have a really sad idea of what heaven will be like. I'm reminded of this every time I hear somebody say, "There better be football in heaven."

I must admit, I don't have a clear window into heaven. I can see why people find treasures in heaven confusing. Money I understand. Money I can account for. With investments, I can choose the options with the highest payout. With expenses, I can choose to spend wisely. That's what accountants are good at. But when it comes to treasures in heaven, it is harder to know what we're shooting for.

The author of Hebrews says, "Now faith is confidence in

what we hope for and assurance about what we do not see" (11:1). Yet many of us do not have "confidence in what we hope for." In fact, most of us have no idea what treasures in heaven look like. How, then, can we pursue treasures in heaven? What are they?

I'm new to this treasure hunt, so I'll stick to the obvious ones. *God* and *people*.

These are the only things that I can think of on earth that have eternal value. And while this may not be the whole list of treasures in heaven, I think it's a pretty good start.

To be sure, the biggest treasure in heaven is God Himself. I'm surprised how many people miss this one. Talk about the elephant in the room. It's like setting out on the old California gold rush without knowing what gold is.

GOD and *people*. These are the only things that I can think of on earth that have eternal value. And while this may not be the whole list of treasures in heaven, I think it's a pretty good start.

On the evening before the crucifixion, Jesus told His disciples that He was going to "prepare a place for you . . . that you also may be where I am" (John 14:3). Those who think treasures in heaven will be gold streets or pearly gates completely miss the point. God—the Creator of the universe, Creator of life, whose glory is so beyond us that it would kill us to see His face in our current earthly forms—will be there. Yes, that God. And He has a place for us. Now we see through a glass, a dim reflection. Then, we will see Him face to face. If you can understand that God created everything you ever wanted, an obvious conclusion given that He created everything that anyone has ever known, let your mind run free long enough to toy with the knowledge that He will be there in person. Not just His works, but He Himself. Bam!

By my calling God the biggest treasure in heaven, you might rightly ask, "How can I have more of God?" How could He be a treasure in heaven?

I can't say I know much about this either, but will use the old adage about what gives real estate its value. "Location. Location. Location." Similarly, the seats closer to the head of the table are prized possessions. Front row seats to the show. And He's the Show! Remember how Jesus' disciples James and John wanted to sit at His right and left side in His kingdom (Matt. 20:20–28)? They even got their momma to ask Jesus for the premium seats. How could Jesus turn down the request of someone's mother? And remember how incensed the other ten disciples were at their request? They understood that proximity to Jesus was big.

Still, my guess is that none of the disciples had any idea of how audacious James and John's request really was. Especially given whose seats they were asking for. You might have missed this, too. Perhaps I'm wrong, but it seems to me that if Jesus is seated at the right hand of God, we know who is seated on Jesus' left.

Yes. Unbeknownst to them, one of them would have taken the Father's seat.

What other treasures will there be in heaven for us? People. Not in the broken state we are in now, but restored as intended. And not just any people. The people you loved enough to invest in them so that they might see Christ in you. People drawn to our Creator by you reflecting His light to the world. Heaven rejoices when one sinner repents and comes to life in Christ, when one lost sheep is found, when a lost son returns to his Father. Peter understood this. In some of his final words, he tells us to

> make every effort to add to your faith goodness; and to
> goodness, knowledge; and to knowledge, self-control;
> and to self-control, perseverance; and to perseverance,
> godliness; and to godliness, mutual affection; and to
> mutual affection, love. . . . For if you do these things, you

will never stumble, and you will receive a rich welcome into the eternal kingdom. (2 Peter 1:5–7, 10–11)

Paul also understood this. He said, "Though I am free and belong to no one, I have made myself a slave to everyone, to win as many as possible" (1 Cor. 9:19). He goes on to say, "Run in such a way as to get the prize" (9:24). Not like the Olympians of his day, for a crown that would not last, but for a crown that will last forever.

Make no mistake about it. While God's divine power has given us everything we need for life and godliness, somehow He includes us in His work. Paul says it this way: "I have become all things to all people so that by all possible means I might save some. I do all this for the sake of the gospel, that I may share in its blessings" (9:22–23). The quality of each of our work will be tested, and, "If what has been built survives, the builder will receive a reward" (1 Cor. 3:14).

So Jesus tells us to be "rich toward God."

Impediments to More

I love how Jesus chose a farmer in His parable of the rich fool. As a farmer, there are three things you can do with seed. Eat it, plant it, or store it. Remarkably like money, by the way. You can use it, invest it, or save it.

The wise farmer plants his surplus seed. When a farmer throws his seed on the ground, he is giving up what he could have eaten. There are risks, and it takes work. But he does so in the hopes of getting more. Undoubtedly there is a time for storing. Prudence dictates that a farmer set aside enough for future contingencies. But how much is enough? Excess seed left in the barn not only forgoes a growing season, but becomes susceptible to rot and rats. Plus, the longer the seed goes without being planted, the less likely it is to germinate.

> **IS IT** wrong to save? To retire? Or to enjoy what God has given you? The answers to these questions start and end with who you love, and who you fear.

In a perfect world, a world without risk, without drought, pestilence, and plunderer, the farmer would plant everything he couldn't eat.

So why don't we do that?

Jesus exposes three impediments that keep us from making the most of what He has given us.

Fear, laziness, and selfishness.

Surveys regularly find that two out of three people are more afraid of running out of money before they die than of death itself.[6] In the passage surrounding the rich fool, Jesus touches on fear over ten times. Specifically, He tells us to get fear right:

> "I tell you, my friends, do not be afraid of those who kill the body and after that can do no more. But I will show you whom you should fear: Fear him who, after your body has been killed, has authority to throw you into hell. Yes, I tell you, fear him." (Luke 12:4–5)

Another reason we don't make the most of what He has given us is laziness. Delayed laziness, perhaps, but laziness just the same. If you're like me, a habitual saver, you might not recognize this in yourself. But we can be poor judges, even of our own motives. Over a dozen times in this passage, Jesus exhorts the crowd to serve. To be dressed, ready, and waiting. To the one who does right, "he will put him in charge of all his possessions" (Luke 12:44). But for the lazy servant who mistreats others and misspends the wealth he is managing on himself, "The master of that servant will come on a day when he does not expect him and at an hour he is not aware of. He will cut him to pieces and assign him a place with the unbelievers" (Luke 12:46).

Finally, selfishness crushes wealth's blessings. The rich

fool thought God's blessing was for himself alone. He didn't understand, or possibly didn't care, that God's blessing was for more than himself. "From everyone who has been given much, much will be demanded; and from the one who has been entrusted with much, much more will be asked" (Luke 12:48).

The "Other Brother" Syndrome

At the end of the day, is it wrong to save? To retire? Or to enjoy what God has given you?

The answers to these questions start and end with who you love, and who you fear.

Jesus reminds us that there are two kinds of fools. It is easy to recognize the fool who lives irresponsibly, like the Prodigal Son. But those of us who are prudent are in danger of the "other brother" syndrome. Like the prodigal's brother (Luke 15:25–32), we see those around us who squander what they've been given, and we are tempted to despise their wasted lives and lack of control. Instead of the father, who daily watches for his lost son's return, like the older brother our hearts turn cold as we dutifully serve. And we become susceptible to that great sin of the Pharisees: *hypocrisy*. We live lives that look good to everyone, but inwardly we are full of greed. We condemn our brother who squanders his early years, all the time longing to squander our later ones. So Jesus warns us, "Be on your guard against the yeast of the Pharisees, which is hypocrisy. There is nothing concealed that will not be disclosed, or hidden that will not be made known" (Luke 12:1–2).

Do you have the heart of your Father? Or of the other brother?

We were made for more. And He is able to do "immeasurably more than all we ask or imagine" (Eph. 3:20) when we align our hearts with His.

8

The Profit Principle

". . . estimate the cost . . ."

LUKE 14:28

I've got to admit, I'm fascinated by fanatics. And apparently I'm not alone. Consider the headlines of any magazine in the supermarket checkout line. Inquiring minds want to know.

My interest in fanatics, however, is not with those on the celebrity list. I'm more interested in the Christian variety of crazy. I'm interested in those who stick out in weird ways, who have done things, said things, championed things, put feet to their faith in ways that are different, even extreme. I can't explain why, exactly. Maybe it's because I'm cautious. I don't want to jump off that bridge until I find out the guy who jumped before me survived. And some of them don't.

But in those moments, we see Jesus.

Nothing moves us more than seeing the depth of Jesus' love for us. That He would give up His life to make a way to His Father.

Yet nothing terrifies us more than when He says that we should do the same. So it is with great fear that we find Jesus' edict:

> And whoever does not carry their cross and follow me cannot be my disciple. Suppose one of you wants to build a tower. Won't you first sit down and estimate the cost to see if you have enough money to complete it? . . . In the same way, those of you who do not give up everything you have cannot be my disciples. (Luke 14:27–28, 33)

NOTHING moves us more than seeing the depth of Jesus' love for us. That He would give up His life to make a way to His Father. Yet nothing terrifies us more than when He says that we should do the same.

His words are so shocking that, consciously or not, we don't seem to hear them. His disciples didn't, either.

By every account, Jesus' disciples were completely blindsided when Jesus was crucified. They thought it was over. First they went into hiding, and then they went back to work. As in fishing. They returned to their old jobs. It wasn't until Jesus appeared to the disciples after His resurrection that they realized that Jesus' death on the cross was all part of the plan.

It's not that His disciples weren't committed. Every one of the twelve apostles had left everything to follow Him. And if He would have asked them to take up their swords, they would have been all in. They were ready to fight to the death. Fight for justice. Oust the Romans. Let the revolution begin! But they didn't know where He would lead them. They had plans of their own for Jesus.

Hindsight being 20/20, we modern-day Christians forget how unfathomable Jesus' words must have been when He said them. He made His cross-carrying statement in real time. That means from His disciples' vantage point, the crucifixion hadn't happened yet. So when Jesus said that for anyone to come after Him, they'd need to get their cross and get in line, it seems to have been so shocking that they simply put it out of their minds.

With hindsight, we have no such luxury.

So while we applaud Jesus for His amazing sacrifice, moved that the Son of God "humbled himself by becoming obedient to death—even death on a cross!" (Phil. 2:8), we secretly wonder how this could be consistent with Jesus' promise, "I have come that they may have life, and have it to the full" (John 10:10b).

We hear Jesus' words, and like so many who turned away from Him at that time, we say, "Jesus, you're asking too much! The cost is too high." If only we knew that in doing so, we make the classic business blunder. We consider the cost without considering the revenue.

The Profit Principle

There are few truths in business. Few principles that always hold. But one exception is the profit equation:

$$Revenue - Cost = Profit$$

What you earn (revenue) minus what you give up to earn it (cost) equals your gain (profit).

This principle holds true for everyone. Everywhere. Everybody knows this.

Yet it is uncanny how often we still separate the two parts of the equation, focusing either on *revenue* or *cost* by itself. And when we do, everything comes crashing down. Like the New Economy. Remember that one? It was the late 1990s, and the Information Age promised to replace the Industrial Age. The rise of technology had everyone buzzing. Dot-com businesses were all the rage, and tech gurus gave speeches to eager investors on how everything we thought we knew about business didn't hold true in the New Economy. The new rule was maximize revenue. Forget about the costs. Superstars like Buy.com were buying books for $10, and selling them for $5. And the more they sold, the happier they were! Their stock prices shot through the roof. So fixated were they on their growing *revenue* that they completely missed that their *costs* were growing even faster. And in a flash, the dot-coms became the dot-bombs. The financial markets collapsed, and the unsuspecting world mourned their losses.

We make the same classic business blunder when we grapple with Jesus' teaching: "In the same way, those of you who do not give up everything you have cannot be my disciples" (Luke 14:33).

We consider the *cost* without the *revenue*. And we think it is too high.

But that is where we go wrong. Yes, the *cost* is high. But it pales in comparison to the *revenue*! And you cannot separate the two. Jesus is offering us the investment of a lifetime, and all we can see is what we give up. And like so many of His followers at that time, we walk away. Or we simply conclude that He couldn't have meant what He said.

But Jesus did know what He was saying.

YES, the *cost* is high. But it pales
in comparison to the *revenue*!

Jesus knew exactly where He was going. To His Father. And the road to get there: via the cross. Jesus knew the cost was very high. So high, in fact, that in a moment of great anguish, "his sweat was like drops of blood falling to the ground" (Luke 22:44). And He cried out to His Father to ask if there was any other way: "Father, if you are willing, take this cup from me; yet not my will, but yours be done" (Luke 22:42).

Yes, Jesus knew the cost was high. But He knew the revenue far outweighed the cost. We need Jesus' perspective:

> For the joy set before him he endured the cross, scorning its shame, and sat down at the right hand of the throne of God. . . . Therefore God exalted him to the highest place and gave him the name that is above every name, that at the name of Jesus every knee should bow, in heaven and on earth and under the earth, and every tongue acknowledge that Jesus Christ is Lord, to the glory of God the Father. (Heb. 12:2; Phil. 2:9–11)

TRUTH:

Following Jesus costs everything we have. But not nearly what He is worth.

The apostle Paul understood this. He was once stoned, three times beaten with rods, and five times given thirty-nine lashes. Still he concluded, "For our light and momentary troubles are achieving for us an eternal glory that far outweighs them all" (2 Cor. 4:17).

And there are those today who also understand. People we call fanatics.

Like Jim Elliot. A lot of you are too young to remember him, but his wife, Elisabeth, captured his story in the book *Through Gates of Splendor*. Jim, along with four other young men, lost his life trying to bring the gospel to the Huarorani people in Ecuador. Before going in, he knew the risks. Jim wrote in his diary, "He is no fool who gives what he cannot keep to gain that which he cannot lose."[7] He was a treasure hunter of another ilk.

Perhaps Jim's story is more personal because my life crossed his in an indirect way. When I was little, I used to love show-and-tell, that classroom ritual where kids bring something from home to present in front of the class. I loved it because I had the best props. Who could compete with a five-inch butterfly decked out in electric blue, or a two-inch beetle bulky enough to pull a Tonka truck? But most glorious of all was the fourteen-foot boa constrictor skin. Split lengthwise, it was more than a foot across. When I rolled that beauty out, I could feel the adulation. I was a six-year-old rock star!

And each of these items came direct from Ecuador. From Jim's part of the world. Because killing Jim didn't stop Christians from going to Ecuador. It emboldened them. People like John and Joyce Stuck (my mom's college roommate), who felt compelled by God to continue the work Jim started.

They were following in Jesus' footsteps, loving others because Jesus loved them. They understood that Jesus' call is meant to enrich us, not impoverish us. They knew that you can't keep anything here, but you can keep everything there. What Randy Alcorn calls the Treasure Principle: "You can't take it with you—but you *can* send it on ahead."[8]

Jesus knows the road looks hard, and that the cost is great. But He also knows the end is worth so much more. Eternity with His Father. And He is worth it. In compassion, He came to show us the road that leads us home.

Consider the cost. But also consider the revenue. Only then will you truly profit.

9

The Giving
Paradox

*"Give to everyone who asks you,
and if anyone takes what belongs
to you, do not demand it back."*

LUKE 6:30

I am torn on how to begin to write about giving.

On the one hand, it is impossible to love without giving. I don't know if you ever thought of love that way before, but it's true. And the greater the love, the greater the gift. As Jesus said, "Greater love has no one than this: to lay down one's life for one's friends" (John 15:13). And He would know. He spoke those words to His friends the night He was betrayed by one of them. Jesus, God in the form of a man, humbled Himself and gave us the greatest gift humanly possible.

Likewise, God the Father gave the greatest gift heavenly possible: "For God so loved the world that he gave his one and only Son" (John 3:16). In case you missed how costly that was, God gave up the one thing He couldn't make more of, His Son, and in doing so not only gave the thing most valued by Him, but silenced His critics who might otherwise claim that any gift from God was of no cost at all, as He could just make more.

So great loving begins with great giving.

On the other hand, I can think of no other thing that has the power to puff a person up like giving. Both in their own eyes and in the eyes of the world. What could be more noble? What could be more selfless? What could be more desired?

Everybody wants to be close to a person who gives gifts. The praise flows. But our quest for praise is dangerous. As Solomon said, "The crucible for silver and the furnace for gold, but people are tested by their praise" (Prov. 27:21). Knowing this, Jesus warned, "When you give to the needy, do not let your left hand know what your right hand is doing" (Matt. 6:3).

Be careful, then, how you give. Because great giving is not necessarily great loving. Paul warned, "If I give all I possess to the poor and give over my body to hardship that I may boast, but do not have love, I gain nothing" (1 Cor. 13:3).

Giving to God

If you ask people what God says about money, most will tell you that He wants you to give it to Him. Everybody's heard "that sermon." It's the excuse some people use for avoiding church altogether. They're afraid they might come on the day "that sermon" is preached. Then they'll have guilt. Or they'll be impoverished. Either way they lose.

> IT is impossible to love without giving . . .
> and the greater the love, the greater the gift . . .
> but great giving is not necessarily great loving.

Even if the pastor doesn't preach on money, sooner or later they'll pass the plate. Awkward. Then you have to avoid eye contact with the bouncers coming down the aisles. There's nowhere to hide. You have to fake like you're really into the worship band. Or the organist. So you're stuck sitting there, wishing you'd thought ahead, like the guy next to you, who stuffed his pocket full of one dollar bills wrapped in a $20. Then you could minimize the damage and get out with your head held high.

But here's a news flash for all you out there who think God wants your money. He doesn't. God does not need your money. God does not want your money.

He wants you. He wants your heart. But He also understands that "money is the answer for everything" (Eccl. 10:19) in that it is the metric we use to quantify our hopes and dreams. When we give money, we're actually giving our time, talents, and treasures, all wrapped up in one. Anytime we give, we give up what we could have used that money for—anything from food to entertainment to a day off work to early retirement. Whatever our heart desires. In giving, we've put someone else's needs ahead of our own. Giving is the cost of our love.

As I mentioned earlier, when I set out to write a book about God's perspective on money, His command to "give to everyone who asks you" knocked me off my high horse and set me on my rear. In fact, at one point all I could hear was "give it all away . . . *give it all away* . . . GIVE IT ALL AWAY!"

How natural it was for me to conclude, then, that my giving is what it's all about. Yet when I classified over 1,300 passages of Scripture into twenty-three categories, our giving didn't even make the top five list of things the Bible says about money. Not "giving to God," not "giving to the poor," nor "giving to others." And nothing could have surprised me more. Giving just *had* to be at the top of the list. I must have missed something. Something had to be wrong with my math. My mind was screaming, "This cannot be!"

IN giving, we've put someone else's needs
ahead of our own. Giving is the cost of our love.

What could possibly have crowded out God's commands
to give? As I looked back over the list, the answer was surprisingly simple.

He did.

God was so busy giving to us that *His* giving crowded out
any amount of giving on our part. God was so busy giving us
everything we need, from here to eternity, that His commands
for us to give are stuck in the back seat. I missed this, because I
was so pent up by Jesus' command for me to "give to everyone
who asks" (Luke 6:30). That command convicted me and left
me stunned. Frozen. Like a deer in the headlights.

How could I be so blind? So deluded? So arrogant? So
slow? So childish? I was so spun up about God's commands for
me to give that I missed the big truth.

TRUTH:

God is the real Giver.

My attitude toward giving reminds me of how my young sons used to respond when I asked them for one of their French fries. You know, the ones I'd just bought them. Under great duress, they would sort through the scraps and find one short enough to spare. That's how I often treat God. Even though all I have comes from Him.

And when we finally do give, we're tempted to perform a victory dance like a rookie running back in the end zone of his first Super Bowl. "Bam, baby! Thank you, Jesus, for making me me!" The truth of the matter is that God doesn't need your money. In fact, there is nothing you have that God needs. In God's eyes, even the richest one among us is dirt poor. "Surely the lowborn are but a breath, the highborn are but a lie. If weighed on a balance, they are nothing" (Ps. 62:9). Any amount of money we have, regardless of how much, when compared to His wealth, is nothing. To put this in mathematical terms, anything divided by infinity is zero.

This is not to say God does not want us to give. Far from it. There are numerous commands for us to give, which fit nicely into three main categories: *giving to God*, *giving to the poor*, and *giving to others.* But we need to take a deeper look at *why* God wants us to give.

Why Give?

"Since God has so much already, why does He ask us to give at all?"

I think that's a fair question. Especially since He doesn't need it. And He knows better than us who does.

From the Scriptures, I see at least three clear reasons God calls us to give: (1) to know Him better, (2) to set us free from Money as a master, and (3) to enrich us.

To Know Him Better

When we give, we come to know God better. To know His character. That He is a giver. That He is *the* Giver. "Every good and perfect gift is from above, coming down from the Father of heavenly lights, who does not change like shifting shadows" (James 1:17). Just as we love Him and others because He first loved us, we also give because He first gave to us. When we give, we reflect His character. When we give as God intended, we more fully understand and know the Lord. The prophet Jeremiah writes,

> This is what the LORD says: "Let not the wise boast of their wisdom or the strong boast of their strength or the rich boast of their riches, but let the one who boasts boast about this: that they have the understanding to know me,

that I am the LORD, who exercises *kindness, justice and righteousness* on earth, for in these I delight," declares the LORD. (Jer. 9:23–24, emphasis added)

Godly giving, then, is *kind*, *just*, or *right*, and oftentimes all three.

How is God's character reflected in our giving? I think it looks something like this.

GOD'S kindness, like His love, has everything to do with His character, and nothing to do with ours.

When we give to "everyone who asks" (Luke 6:30), we show God's *kindness*. Kind giving has nothing to do with the recipient's merit. Kind giving is what Jesus refers to when He says that His Father "is kind to the ungrateful and wicked" (Luke 6:35), that He "causes his sun to rise on the evil and the good, and sends rain on the righteous and the unrighteous" (Matt. 5:45). God's kindness, like His love, has everything to do with His character, and nothing to do with ours.

When we give to those who merit our gift, we show God's *justice*. Just giving is what God does when He blesses those who walk in His ways.

> Blessed is the one who does not walk in step with the wicked or stand in the way that sinners take or sit in the company of mockers, but whose delight is in the law of the Lord, and who meditates on his law day and night. That person is like a tree planted by streams of water, which yields its fruit in season and whose leaf does not wither—whatever they do prospers. (Ps.1:1–3)

When we give to the poor, fatherless, widow, and foreigner, we show God's *righteousness*. Right giving sees those in need, and meets their needs. Jesus tells us,

> "So do not worry, saying, 'What shall we eat?' or 'What shall we drink?' or 'What shall we wear?' For the pagans run after all these things, and your heavenly Father knows that you need them. But seek first his kingdom and his righteousness, and all these things will be given to you as well." (Matt. 6:31–33)

When we feed and clothe the poor, fatherless, widow, and foreigner, through His wisdom, we join the Defender of the Weak and give what is right.

Godly giving brings glory to God. Looking after widows and orphans in their distress (James 1:27), clothing and feeding those in need, forgiving as we have been forgiven, are all ways to "let your light shine before others, that they may see your good deeds and glorify your Father in heaven" (Matt. 5:16).

I was pondering all this while sitting on a bench in Sydney's Chinatown, just outside Paddy's Market, when a man about sixty years old, missing teeth and smelling of the street, sat down next to me. "I prayed to Jesus for a place to stay, and I got one," he said. And I praised God. Sydney is an expensive city. God answers our prayers. He is kind. He is just. He is righteous.

To Set Us Free

God also asks us to give to set us free from the false master Money. In case you think that slavery is dead, understand the words of Peter, that "people are slaves to whatever has mastered them" (2 Peter 2:19). By giving, you physically trade the promises offered by Money for the promises offered by God.

Giving is the antidote to greed and the deceitfulness of wealth. Greed, the inordinate desire to obtain wealth to keep for oneself, is idolatry. Giving has a way of freeing us from Money as master. By giving, we remember who it was who gave us all we have and are, and with a generous spirit we respond with gratitude to God for His provision to us and look to give as He gave.

> BY giving, we remember who it was who gave us all we have and are, and with a generous spirit we respond with gratitude to God for His provision to us and look to give as He gave.

Abraham understood the ties of wealth. In response to the king of Sodom's offer to keep the spoils of battle recovered when he rescued his nephew Lot along with the kings of Sodom and Gomorrah where Lot lived, he said, "With raised hand I have sworn an oath to the LORD, God Most High, Creator of heaven and earth, that I will accept nothing belonging to you, not even a thread or the strap of a sandal, so that you will never be able to say, 'I made Abram rich'" (Gen. 14:22–23). He wanted no bond to this kingdom that God would later destroy because of its wickedness.

To Enrich Us

Finally, God wants us to give to enrich us, not to impoverish us. The math seems so terribly wrong on this one that it is easy to miss this principle altogether. So here's the "red letter" version:

"The Lord Jesus himself said: 'It is more blessed to give than to receive'" (Acts 20:35).

You can't get any more direct than that. But we don't believe Him. If we really believed Him, we'd try as hard to give as we try to receive. Instead, we treat giving to God like a tax. The cost of being a Christian. And like a good citizen, we pay up. But not without looking for loopholes.

Take the tithe, for example. Literally a tenth, it's pretty easy to do the math. "Did God want me to give a tenth of everything? Or just my income? And was that 10 percent of adjusted gross income, or taxable income? Because I've got a lot of deductions this year." The arguments go on and on. We apparently view 10 percent as an upper boundary. And we're getting worse, not better. A study by Empty Tomb found that church giving by members decreased from 3.11 percent of income in 1968 to 2.43 percent in 2008.[9]

There are even arguments in the church today on whether the tithe applies to the New Testament church at all, or if it can be discarded as an Old Testament command. But why do we ask this question? Is it because we want to hold on to all that we can?

The tithe did not start out as a command at all. Rather, it was Abraham's (then named Abram) joyful response to the blessing he'd received from Melchizedek, king of Salem and priest of God Most High.

WE treat giving to God like a tax. The cost of being a Christian. And like a good citizen, we pay up. But not without looking for loopholes.

Abram met Melchizedek on his return home from winning a battle to rescue his nephew Lot. And he'd won against terrible odds. With only 318 men, he crushed the armies of five kings who had just wiped out four other kings, including the kings of Sodom and Gomorrah, where Lot lived. Abram recovered his nephew along with the captives and all their goods. On Abram's trek home, Melchizedek greeted him and blessed him, and Abram gave credit where credit was due by giving a tenth of all he had to the priest. This was in addition to returning all the plunder to the king of Sodom.

So the tithe was initially an expression of gratefulness to God. Only later through the Law of Moses did God make the tithe a command, to care for the priesthood (Levites), who had no inheritance in the Promised Land except for God alone, and to also fill the storehouses to feed the poor, widows, fatherless, and foreigners who dwelled in their land.

God even tells us to test Him on this: "'Bring the whole tithe into the storehouse, that there may be food in my house. Test me in this,' says the LORD Almighty, 'and see if I will not throw open the floodgates of heaven and pour out so much blessing that there will not be room enough to store it'" (Mal. 3:10).

If only we really believed God when He says, "It is more blessed to give than to receive."

How deceived we are! God wants to enrich us, and we think He is trying to impoverish us! He knows that worldly wealth is the lesser blessing—that we can't take it with us, but we can send it on ahead. That somehow we can trade what we can't keep for what we can't lose. This is God's way. And it is so much beyond ours.

TRUTH:

It really is more blessed to give than to receive.

Paul spells this out clearly in his letter commending the Philippians for their generosity in helping him while in need. "Not that I desire your gifts; what I desire is that more be credited to your account" (Phil. 4:17).

How is it possible that we miss this?

How else can I say this? We are blind and bewitched! We live our lives as bewildered alchemists, turning gold into lead. Unless we realize our impoverished state, we have no part in Him. We need to understand that apart from God, we are poor, regardless of how we stack up against our neighbor. Only when we realize our true position can we hear Jesus' words, "Blessed are the poor in spirit, for theirs is the kingdom of heaven" (Matt. 5:3). As we look forward to His kingdom, Jesus encourages us to put our treasures there. To put our hearts there. With Him.

> **AS** we look forward to His kingdom, Jesus encourages us to put our treasures there. To put our hearts there. With Him.

God is a giver. Giving aligns our hearts with His. We love Him because He first loved us (1 John 4:19).

Consider those questions I had the first day Jesus' terrifying advice ruined the book I planned to write.

1. Can I give too much?

Apparently not. Jesus commended the widow who gave her last two coins—all she had to live on (Mark 12:41–44). And then there is the widow of Zarephath (1 Kings 17:7–16). She fed the prophet Elijah, even as she and her son were picking up sticks to build a fire and cook their last meal before they lay down to die of starvation. God rewarded her generosity, and her oil and flour did not run out.

God, increase our faith.

2. Can I give to the wrong person?

Apparently not. God gives to everyone. The righteous and the wicked.

3. Can I give irresponsibly?

Apparently yes. While God gives every one of us everything we have, He does not give anyone everything they ask for. Not even the apostle Paul, who prayed three times to be healed. Not even Jesus, who prayed, "Father, if it is possible, may this cup be taken from me. Yet not as I will, but as you will" (Matt. 26:39). Not even in a perfect world, like in the garden, before the fall.

God does not give what is outside His will, does not give what is second best, and does not give what He has specifically prohibited. He does not give that we may glorify ourselves, to spend on our pleasures, or for our arrogance and boasting.

Lingering Questions

After reading and rereading God's directives on giving, I still have a lot of questions. I still don't have an answer for Jack and his mountain bike. And I still don't know if I should give to that guy on the street corner. On the one hand, Jesus says to give to everyone who asks you, and God Himself gives His rain and sun on the wicked and the good.

On the other hand, He does not give everyone everything they ask. He especially doesn't give bad gifts. Or gifts for bad purposes. James 4:3 says, "When you ask, you do not receive, because you ask with wrong motives, that you may spend what you get on your pleasures." Paul gave the following rule, "The one who is unwilling to work shall not eat" (2 Thess. 3:10). Likewise, Agur observes, "Under three things the earth trembles, under four it cannot bear up," one of them being "a godless fool who gets plenty to eat" (Prov. 30:21–22).

My tentative conclusion is to err on the side of mercy. And pray for wisdom.

Which leads to the most important question for a life well lived.

How should we then give?

10

The Great Exchange

"I tell you, use worldly wealth to gain friends for yourselves, so that when it is gone, you will be welcomed into eternal dwellings."

LUKE 16:9

Once we really believe "it is more blessed to give than to receive," it completely changes our view of giving. The question changes from, "How much must I give?" to "How much can I give?" When we truly understand God's view of giving, we see the wisdom of Paul's advice, "Whoever sows sparingly will also reap sparingly" (2 Cor. 9:6). Then we want to plant a big field.

So, if you're fully convinced of the excellence of the investment, you're ready for the quest of a lifetime: "How do I maximize my eternal net worth?" Imagine if you were playing Monopoly, and you were offered the chance to trade in your pink fivers for real ones. Or better yet, trade the yellow $100 Monopoly bills in for Benjamins. You'd go straight to the bank and make the exchange. And you wouldn't ask how many of the Monopoly bills you could keep. You'd trade in every last one.

In Jesus' parable of the shrewd manager (Luke 16), He tells us how to do exactly that—trade in the fake for the real. We can swap what we can't keep for what we can. Jesus describes a manager who was caught wasting the rich owner's wealth. The owner demands an account, and the manager quickly makes several shady side deals with his master's debtors to assure he'll land on his feet in a new position once he's fired from his current one.

Jesus concludes the parable this way:

"The master commended the dishonest manager because he had acted shrewdly. For the people of this world are more shrewd in dealing with their own kind than are the people of the light. I tell you, use worldly wealth to gain friends for yourselves, so that when it is gone, you will be welcomed into eternal dwellings." (Luke 16:8–9)

As usual, Jesus' words take us by surprise. We tend to get hung up on the manager's dishonesty and the owner commending

142

him for it. It seems more likely to us that the defrauded owner would take his manager out and flog him. Or whatever they did back then.

But Jesus is giving us a clear window into how to be truly rich—how to accumulate treasures in heaven. Friends in heaven. He's already commanded that we do this—to store up treasures in heaven. But here He is telling us directly how to do so.

> WILL you "make every effort" to build on
> the foundation of faith, and "receive a rich
> welcome into the eternal kingdom"
> (2 Peter 1:5, 11), or arrive a pauper, "as one
> escaping through the flames" (1 Cor. 3:15)?

"I tell you, use worldly wealth to gain friends for yourselves, so that when it is gone, you will be welcomed into eternal dwellings" (Luke 16:9).

If you listen closely, you'll see how similar this advice is to what Jesus told the rich young ruler. "Go, sell everything you have and give to the poor, and you will have treasure in heaven" (Mark 10:21). Trade what you can't keep for eternal treasures.

Every person who receives the grace and peace offered by God the Father through His Son, Jesus, needs to know that this is just the beginning of life. But what comes next? Will you "make every effort" to build on the foundation of faith, and "receive a rich welcome into the eternal kingdom" (2 Peter 1:5, 11), or arrive a pauper, "as one escaping through the flames" (1 Cor. 3:15)?

Jesus explains how we can make the most of the lives He has given us. And being God, of course He does it much more succinctly than I ever could.

Maximizing Your Eternal Net Worth

Jesus follows up the parable about the shrewd manager with a clear path for eternal treasures. How to use worldly wealth to gain BFFs—best friends forever.

> "Whoever can be trusted with very *little* can also be trusted with very *much*, and whoever is *dishonest* with very little will also be dishonest with much. So if you have not been *trustworthy* in handling *worldly wealth*, who will trust you with *true riches*? And if you have not been trustworthy with *someone else's property*, who will give you *property of your own*?" (Luke 16:10–12, emphasis added)

In a few short verses, Jesus explains how to be truly rich. The path leads from little to much, worldly wealth to true riches, stewardship ("someone else's property") to ownership ("property of your own"). And it is laid on the foundation of trustworthiness.

We maximize our eternal net worth by being trustworthy, from little to much, worldly wealth to true treasures, stewardship to ownership.

Dishonest to Trustworthy

If you want to know how to fail, I'm your guy. In fact, I wrote my dissertation on the topic. Bankruptcy prediction modeling, to be precise. And after looking at every publicly traded company that failed over two decades, I can tell you with great confidence that failure is not that hard. Anybody can do it.

While there are many ways to fail financially, my personal favorites are the frauds. Enron, WorldCom, AIG. Companies too big to fail until the public realized they were too fake to survive. But by then the damage was done. These cases highlight the infamous deceivers of our time, and their names are briefly in the press and on our minds, yet quickly forgotten. Does anybody remember Jeffrey Skilling, CEO of Enron? Or Scotty Sullivan, CFO of WorldCom? Or their companies, for that matter?

Sometimes we forget so quickly that we allow them to do it again. Barry Minkow fits into this category. As an eighteen-year-old, Barry became the darling of American capitalism by starting ZZZZ Best, a commercial carpet-cleaning and restoration business so successful that soon his company was publicly traded on the New York Stock Exchange, the biggest exchange in the world. By the time he was twenty-one, Barry's company had grown to where his share alone was worth over $100 million. But there was one little problem. His company wasn't real. In fact, ZZZZ Best never restored even one carpet. Instead, his employees spent all their time faking it. Faking customers, faking sales, faking bills. They were so good at it that they deceived one of the biggest audit firms in the world, going to such lengths as to print signs in front of downtown office buildings they were supposed to be servicing, and bribing night guards to "recognize" them as they brought auditors by to inspect the carpet restorations they weren't actually doing.

Unfortunately, all good things must come to an end. And Barry's end included a twenty-five-year trip to a US penitentiary. While there, Barry checked out Christianity, admittedly at first to get a lighter sentence, but later because he was amazed by God's mercy. He knew he was a sinner and knew he needed to be reformed. While under lock and key, Barry got a new start on life, and went so far as to earn an online degree in Christian ministry. He became more than a model prisoner. He put his old skills at deception to good use, or rather, use for good. From prison, Barry assisted the FBI in case after case, proving that nobody can spot a fraud like a fraud.

Because of his service, Barry was released early. And this time, he steered clear of the financial markets. Far clear. In fact, he became the pastor of the Community Bible Church in San Diego. Twenty years after ZZZZ Best's implosion, Barry was a new man. At forty he had a new life, new wife, new family, new calling. And he made the most of his new opportunities. His church grew fivefold, and he had a successful side practice uncovering financial fraud.

In 2010, Barry made national headlines again. Seems he began to use his exposés of corporate financial shenanigans to his own benefit, betting in the financial markets against those he accused. His return to federal prison owing over $500 million in restitution serves as a spectacular reminder of the proverb, "As a dog returns to its vomit, so fools repeat their folly" (Prov. 26:11).

With examples like Barry, it's easy to convince ourselves that we're not so bad. We are tempted to believe that deceitfulness related to wealth is the rich guy's problem. Not us little guys, just trying to scrape by.

But Jesus doesn't see it that way. He knows that deception and greed are not limited to the rich and infamous.

He knows that guys like Dennis Kozlowski, former CEO of Tyco, earning more than $100 million per year, didn't start by dodging $1 million in taxes on the Picassos he had just purchased for $10 million. Dennis just got big enough to get noticed. God knows that the temptation to deceive is right there with all of us, great or small.

The US Air Force Academy understood this concept with their honor code: "We will not lie, cheat, steal or tolerate among us those who do."[10] One offense and you were kicked out of the Academy. There was quite the history and folklore around the code, with stories that even included getting kicked out for lying on a date. As a new faculty member there, and the token civilian one at that, suddenly I was thinking about that box of candy I liked to sneak into the movie theater, even though it was clearly posted on the cinema doors, "No outside food or drink allowed."

But their prices were ridiculous, I rationalized.

The ability to rationalize that what you're doing is okay is one of three key ingredients to any fraud, researchers tell us. According to the Fraud Triangle, a person needs three things to commit fraud—opportunity, incentive, and the ability to rationalize that it is okay.[11] For me, the high prices were the rationalization.

Is Dennis Kozlowski so different from me? Sure, he could afford the taxes. But then I could afford to pay twice the price for candy in the movie theater rather than sneaking it in, too.

I just didn't want to. So I cheated. Just a little. And I'd gotten comfortable with it.

Are you trustworthy? Daniel rose to oversee two empires under three very disparate kings, because he was "trustworthy and neither corrupt nor negligent" (Dan. 6:4). And in doing so, two of those kings changed their edict from "Worship me only" to "Worship Daniel's God only." I've got a pretty strong suspicion that Daniel has a lot of treasures in heaven. A rich welcome from those who knew God because he was trustworthy.

> JESUS begins with a foundation of
> trustworthiness. He knows that with
> money, there are dangers at every turn.

Abraham, Job, and Joseph serve as godly examples of those who put God first and brought glory to Him through their wealth. Abraham and Job owned their wealth. Joseph and Daniel managed the wealth of kings. Each one brought glory to God through their actions.

But this certainly isn't always the case. In fact, quite often the opposite is true. Paul famously warned that "the love of money is a root of all kinds of evil" (1 Tim. 6:10). That is why Jesus begins with a foundation of trustworthiness. He knows that with money, there are dangers at every turn.

We can even be dishonest when we give. The most sobering example of this involves Ananias and Sapphira, who in the early days of the church were struck dead for conspiring together to lie about the gift they brought from selling a piece of property (Acts 5). Their gift was for show—for their glory, instead of for God's—and He made an example out of their hypocrisy. Of such gifts, Jesus had earlier warned, "you will have no reward from your Father in heaven" (Matt. 6:1).

So be trustworthy.

Little to Much

Next, be faithful with the little you do have. It is easy to imagine that if you had a lot, then you'd really make a difference. But Jesus says otherwise. And so do statistics. Those who get rich quick, from lottery winners to pro athletes, are highly likely to be broke within five years, with nothing to show for it.

The solution? Baby steps. "Whoever can be trusted with very little can also be trusted with very much" (Luke 16:10) Proverbs states, "Whoever gathers money little by little makes it grow" (13:11). That's why tithing and giving, no matter your income, is so important. If you can learn to live off of little, you'll be better prepared to live with much. The same is true with giving. If you can learn to give off of little, you'll be better prepared to give with much.

> **IT** is easy to imagine that if you had a lot,
> then you'd really make a difference. But
> Jesus says otherwise. And so do statistics.

In your eagerness to give, make sure you don't skip these early steps. If you won't share when you have little, odds are you won't share when you have much. Greed doesn't limit itself to one tax bracket.

Begin with handling the little you have right.

Worldly Wealth to True Riches

From my vantage point as a seasoned accounting professor, I see kids show up at college looking pretty good. Just like adults, without the wrinkles. They can feed, clothe, and burp themselves remarkably well. Arguably, too well in some cases. But when they graduate a few years later with all the wisdom of the world packed into their enormous craniums, they still bear a remarkable resemblance to a baby. Little body, big head.

For the first time, they're on their own, making their own decisions, living like grown-ups. Many want to do something meaningful with their lives. To make a difference. But it's hard to give up the lifestyle to which they've grown accustomed. And that lifestyle was built on somebody else's money—most likely that of parents, banks, or the government.

Suddenly, there are bills to pay. They want to be generous, but you can't give what you don't have. That's why Jesus says, "If you have not been trustworthy in handling worldly wealth, who will trust you with true riches?" (Luke 16:11). Some people, eager to give, want to skip this step altogether. They're what I call "Robin Hood Givers." Those who take from the rich and give to the poor. Why wait to give your money when you can give someone else's?

When I was growing up, Dad bought some land, brought in utilities, and rented spaces for a couple manufactured homes. It seemed like a great idea, consistent with his primary investment strategy of buying raw land and putting something income-producing on it. The upside was that the tenants couldn't destroy his rental house; it was their manufactured home, not his. The downside was that low-income housing attracted a less-financially-stable tenant. Over the years, he carried various tenants along month after month, those who for whatever reason couldn't afford to pay the rent.

One such tenant, behind in nearly a year's rent, came by to

explain why he couldn't pay that month. His wife, he explained, was tremendously generous. She had recently flown down South to see their son graduate from boot camp, and when a friend wanted to accompany her but couldn't afford the ticket, his wife stepped up and bought it for her.

When the tenant finished telling his benevolent tale, Dad shrugged. "Kind of feels like I'm the one who bought the tickets."

Giving money you don't have isn't generosity. It's theft.

So hang on to your desire to be generous. But get the order right. Worldly wealth to true riches.

Stewardship to Ownership

Jesus' final step for using worldly wealth to gain friends forever moves from stewardship to ownership. Right handling of "someone else's property" precedes "property of your own." Some Christians like to point out that ultimately God owns everything. And yes, that's true. But they'd still get upset if you drove off with their car. Yes, ultimately everything comes from God. And ultimately, we could do nothing without what God has given us. Our strengths, our talents, our very lives all come from Him. Still, He has given us ownership of some things, and stewardship of others.

Simply put, *stewardship* has to do with handling someone else's money, whereas *ownership* has to do with handling your own money. Stewardship encompasses everything in the Bible from manager to administrator to servant to slave. In today's environment, think employee. Anything from waiting tables to CEO. Ownership ranges from farmers to kings in the Bible, with the modern-day equivalent running from entrepreneur to retiree. Anywhere you make the final call.

Both stewardship and ownership have their challenges. For example, I steward a multimillion-dollar endowment for Christian accounting ethics in the LP and Timothy Leung School of Accounting at Azusa Pacific University. The Leung family's gift is not mine to spend as I see fit. Even if I see a great opportunity to advance God's kingdom, like feeding widows or orphans. Instead, my responsibility is the highest and best use of these assets to make the biggest impact possible within the parameters agreed upon with the donor.

With my own money, I face an additional set of challenges. As owner, it is now my responsibility to determine the highest and best use of my resources to the praise and glory of God. I am unrestricted by anyone else's wishes. But to make the biggest impact, it takes wisdom. So God gives us training wheels. "Someone else's property" to "property of your own."

My friend Rod runs a bug business. He makes traps to catch yellow jackets, wasps, flies, and similar animals that most people find offensive. After thirty years, he's gotten pretty good at it, and he now employs over a hundred people. With his rise in prominence, he finds himself frequently invited to attend Christian events with a range of interests.

At a recent gathering for entrepreneurs, he realized that of about a hundred participants, he was the only one there who wasn't running a nonprofit. It wasn't long until word got around, and he became the most popular guy in the room. Everyone, it seemed, was interested in letting him know how he could participate with them in their venture.

One startup was creating jobs in Africa by employing low-skilled workers there to assemble bicycles. The business plan called for parts to be shipped from the United States to Africa, where the workers would assemble the bicycles and ship them back to sell in the States. Brilliant! With a plan like that, they were sure to remain a nonprofit for the life of the company, however short that may be.

"Nonprofit for Jesus?" Rod questioned. "How about somebody run a for-profit for Jesus?"

Ownership isn't easy. Most startup businesses fail. Nonprofit startups are rumored to fail even faster. Those who do thrive are faced with even greater responsibilities. More people look to you for their livelihood. Will they see in you the Father's kindness, justice, and righteousness?

Many of us won't fully reach the ownership stage until retirement, that final frontier where we take charge of the rest of our lives. What will you do when God removes the last barrier to serving Him alone?

Having spent the last twenty-five years working with students, I am convinced that the next generation depends on godly examples of those who finish strong. Mom warned me that growing old wasn't for sissies long before she faced the frailties God currently has for her. And I will remember her love for Him long after He brings her home. God wants to complete us, and that process takes a lifetime. Finish the race. Own well.

Godlike Giving

Don't be discouraged if it seems like you have nothing to give. Because you do. We often think about giving in relation to money, yet Jesus almost never gave that. Probably because He had much better things to give. I also suspect He didn't want money to get the credit for the things that ultimately come from His Father.

Jesus often gave what money couldn't buy. Like healing, sight, freedom from demons, and recovery from disease. He even gave some back their dead. Or their life. And He offered even more. More than what people knew to ask for. Like living water to those who only wanted H_2O. Or the Bread of Life to those who only wanted bread.

In the same way, Jesus has given His Spirit to those who follow Him, and each of us has received spiritual gifts given to us for the common good (1 Corinthians 12–13). When we use these gifts, we show others the love He has shown us, to the praise and glory of God. And so Jesus tells us, "If anyone gives even a cup of cold water to one of these little ones who is my disciple, truly I tell you, that person will certainly not lose their reward" (Matt. 10:42). And if it comes to money, apparently amount doesn't matter. Of all those putting money into the temple treasury (Mark 12:41–44), it was the poor widow alone who Jesus called out for her generosity, for she put in "all she had to live on."

One of the greatest gifts of all that Jesus gave us was forgiveness. And something that all Christians can give, because of the forgiveness we ourselves have received.

> **JESUS** often gave what money couldn't buy. Like living water to those who only wanted H_2O. Or the Bread of Life to those who only wanted bread.

My friend Steve is one of the foremost experts in forensic accounting. No, he doesn't deal with dead accountants. He provides expert testimony in the courts quantifying the monetary damages due a plaintiff. In his professional role, he frequently sees Christians and how they behave in court related to disputes about money. His conclusion from years of experience? Christians need to be willing to be radically wronged. Few things are more detrimental to the gospel than watching two Christians fighting over worldly wealth. In matters of justice and wealth, he confirms the advice to the Corinthians from Paul, who was appalled that "one brother takes another to court—and this in front of unbelievers! The very fact that you have lawsuits among you means you have been completely defeated already. Why not rather be wronged? Why not rather be cheated?" (1 Cor. 6:6–7).

Giving up your claim to justice, especially when you are in the right, is the essence of forgiveness. And in doing so, you rightly acknowledge that God is sovereign. There is a righteous Judge who will reward you according to what you have done.

It was 2:00 a.m. and the jet's cabin was dark but for the glow of scattered monitors reflecting off a dozen sleeping faces. Still, I shielded my eyes in the cups of my hands to hide the tears rolling down my cheeks. Trying to adjust to the time zone change between LA and Sydney, I had stumbled onto a recent movie adaption of *Les Miserables*, the story of a man named Jean Valjean in eighteenth-century France, interned in a brutal prison work-camp for stealing bread, his humanity reduced to a number—24601—under the harsh treatment of a ruthless guard. When he was finally released, he repaid a priest's kindness of food and shelter by stealing the monastery's silver, and was again caught by the same policeman who said Valjean would never amount to anything. But the priest, practicing Jesus' upside-down words about giving, covered over Valjean's theft and offered instead the remainder of the silver and forgiveness as well.

And as I watched the familiar story unfold, it cut me to the quick. So five miles high and another three thousand miles from the nearest land, surrounded by three hundred sleeping people I did not know nor would I ever see again, I silently wept as I was reminded all over again of God's great mercy and grace in my life. Jean Valjean is me, a faceless man in a world of billions, in need of God's love and forgiveness.

Years ago, a young man in our Bible study asked, "Do I need to forgive someone if they don't ask for forgiveness?" This young man, perhaps the brightest student I've ever had, was torn up inside because of a huge weight on his shoulders. He blamed his mother for the suicide of his brother, because of the impossibly high expectations she put on him. Certainly if any young man was asked to keep up with Donovan (not his real name), the task would have been impossible. In response to his question, I pointed to two examples, the one mentioned earlier of Jesus on the cross, and the other of Stephen, who forgave those stoning Him even as they did so (Acts 7).

Forgiveness is giving. It is giving up your rightful claim against another for an injustice perpetrated against you, and releasing the matter to God, the only wise Judge. And it costs you something—your claim to be made whole, to be compensated for the wrong. Your claim to justice. When we give up that claim, we are showing the love to that person that God has shown to us. He gave up His Son, and gave us forgiveness, before we'd even asked.

We can forgive anyone, regardless of their request for it. To receive forgiveness, however, it seems to me the offending party must ask. Just as we must ask God for forgiveness to be made whole, even though He has already offered it.

> **WHATEVER** wrongs have been perpetrated against us pale in comparison to the offenses we ourselves have committed against a holy God.

What is our position as Christians? We forgive as we have been forgiven. To do otherwise is to withhold the grace we ourselves have received, and in so much greater magnitude. Because whatever wrongs have been perpetrated against us pale in comparison to the offenses we ourselves have committed against a holy God. When we forgive, we experience God's forgiveness fully. Jesus said, "For if you forgive other people when they sin against you, your heavenly Father will also forgive you. But if you do not forgive others their sins, your Father will not forgive your sins" (Matt. 6:14–15).

I freely admit I don't understand how this works. I thought God had to forgive me—that that was in the contract. So I return to my mantra, my fail-safe position, that if my theology disagrees with God, one of us is wrong, and it's not Him.

God's ways are so much higher than ours. He gave us everything we have, without us asking for it. And when we messed it up, He gave us forgiveness, without us paying for it. To top it off, He tells us how we can trade our useless treasures for ones that will last. This is the great exchange.

11

Turning Terrible
to Terrific

*"Blessed are the poor in spirit,
for theirs is the kingdom of heaven."*

MATTHEW 5:3

N ow is our time to walk as Jesus did. More often than not, this begins with money, simply because it measures so many of our hopes and fears. To a world that doesn't recognize Jesus as God's Son, His teachings on money are terrible, in the sense that they are "strongly repulsive; notably unattractive and objectionable."[12]

But to those who do know Him, Jesus' words are a different kind of terrible. "Terrifying" and "awesome." Terrifying, because His advice ruins the empty lives we've planned for ourselves. Awesome, because He replaces our lives with better ones than we could have ever imagined. This book only scratches the surface of Jesus' teachings, but here are ten truths that give us a glimpse of how God does this.

TEN TRUTHS THAT
TURN TERRIBLE TO TERRIFIC

Truth #1: PURPOSE. Jesus' sole purpose on earth was to glorify His Father. Unless we align our purpose with His, our lives will be meaningless. But when we have His purpose, Jesus' terrible financial advice turns from "objectionable" to "awesome."

Truth #2: PRACTICE. Jesus meant every word He said. In the order He taught it, from "turn the other cheek" to "forgive as you have been forgiven," He lived His teachings to the fullest. What would it look like if you followed Jesus' financial advice? In a worst-case scenario, you might end up looking like Him.

Truth #3: MASTER. Money, as an idol, steals God's glory. Who do you love? And who do you fear? Your answer determines your true master.

Truth #4: GOOD. Anything other than God is the wrong "good" thing. We come to Jesus with what we think we need, and He redirects us to His Father. Even the best dreams, like the rich young ruler's quest for eternal life, are the wrong good thing. What is good about eternal life is not the length, but the company.

Truth #5: DECEPTION. We are deceived whenever we think we have a better plan for our lives than God does. Wealth is a blessing, but it becomes a curse for us when we set our hearts on it instead of Him.

Truth #6: JUSTICE. There is a wisdom-wealth connection: do something, do it right, and be generous. Choose wisdom over wealth, because wealth is the lesser blessing. It is just money.

Truth #7: PROSPERITY. God made us for more. More than ourselves, and more than this world. What will you do if God prospers you? Will you have the heart of the prodigal's father, longing for his lost son's return? Or the spiteful heart of his brother? Hypocrisy masks a proper fool, and fear, laziness, and selfishness keep us from being "rich toward God."

Truth #8: PROFIT. Following Jesus costs everything we have. But not nearly what He's worth. Jesus offers us the investment of a lifetime—to trade empty lives for eternal ones—and we think it costs too much. Only when we compare the cost to the revenue can we truly profit.

Truth #9: GIVE. God is the real Giver. It really is more blessed to give than to receive. Jesus commands us to give to reflect His Father's character, doing what is kind, just, and right. He wants to enrich us, not impoverish us, and to set us free from Money as master. *Litmus Test: Do we try as hard to give as to get?*

Truth #10: REWARD. Maximize your eternal net worth by being trustworthy, from little to much, worldly wealth to true treasures, stewardship to ownership. You can trade what you can't keep for eternal treasures. And while you can't give what you don't have, every Christian can give what we need most. Forgiveness.

What will you do with Jesus' terrible financial advice?

Jesus opened His most famous sermon with, "Blessed are the poor in spirit" (Matt. 5:3a). Only when we recognize our true state can we hear Jesus. We are poor. We may claim, "I am rich; I have acquired wealth and do not need a thing," but Jesus responds, "you do not realize that you are wretched, pitiful, poor, blind and naked" (Rev. 3:17). When faced with the holiness of God, there is only one fitting posture. Humility. From Job (10:15) to Isaiah (6:5), all cry out, "Woe to me!"

But when we recognize our extreme poverty, God, in His great mercy, lifts us up with an amazing blessing. We are blessed to receive "the kingdom of heaven" (Matt. 5:3). John explains,

"Yet to all who did receive him, to those who believed in his name, he gave the right to become children of God" (John 1:12).

ONLY when we recognize our true state can we hear Jesus. We are poor. We may claim, "I am rich; I have acquired wealth and do not need a thing," but Jesus responds, "you do not realize that you are wretched, pitiful, poor, blind and naked" (Rev. 3:17).

If you love Him, you will obey His commands (John 14:15). We must not claim His name without claiming His life. To do so is hypocrisy, that two-faced deception that glorifies us as we dishonor God. It may fool our friends, but never Him. The Father sees what is done in secret, and rewards you. In the end, it doesn't matter if you say you know Jesus. It matters if He says He knows you. The saddest words Jesus will ever speak are, "I never knew you. Away from me, you evildoers" (Matt. 7:23).

A Final Paradox

In a society where we have taken independence, individual freedom, and self-love to cult status, submission is taboo. We want to be our own master. Money offers us what we want, so we love it or fear it, trading in the true God for a false one. But Jesus shows us we have it all wrong. He shows us that submission to His Father is the only way to be truly free. Free to live life to the full. The only way to live a life that matters is to find our sole purpose in Him.

I don't know if you've recognized it or not, but Jesus' greatest act of love for us was His greatest act of submission to the will of the Father. On the night He gave up his life for ours, He prayed, "Father, if you are willing, take this cup from me; yet not my will, but yours be done" (Luke 22:42). Jesus saw in front of Him a brutal death, with the upcoming physical suffering surpassed only by the weight of the world's sin that He would bear while dying. Knowing this, He was sweating blood. How could His Father ask for such obedience? Or bear to let Him die? But in submitting to the Father's will, Jesus showed that He obeyed Him in all things. In doing so, He revealed a great mystery. Submission is the flip side of love.

Rather than diminishing who Jesus was, His submission to the Father's will magnified Him. Just as Jesus, through faith, knew that it would. He endured the cross, scorning its shame, for the joy of returning to the right hand of His Father (Heb. 12:2). As He prayed the night He was betrayed, "And now,

Father, glorify me in your presence with the glory I had with you before the world began" (John 17:5). And the Father, as always, proved Himself trustworthy.

THE only way to live a life that matters is to find our sole purpose in Him.

Therefore God exalted him to the highest place and gave him the name that is above every name, that at the name of Jesus every knee should bow, in heaven and on earth and under the earth, and every tongue acknowledge that Jesus Christ is Lord, to the glory of God the Father. (Phil. 2:9–11)

Earlier that night, Jesus called His disciples together for a final meal. Knowing He was returning to His Father, He gave them the following instructions: "You call me 'Teacher' and 'Lord,' and rightly so, for that is what I am. . . . I have set you an example that you should do as I have done for you. . . . Now that you know these things, you will be blessed if you do them"

(John 13:13, 15, 17). His words are as true for us as they were for them.

There is only one true God. And only one true Son. For every situation in which we find ourselves, Jesus remains the only way to the Father. Are you rich in the eyes of the world? Don't go away sad, as the rich young ruler did. Choose the right "good" thing.

Are you exceedingly poor, with a net worth and self-worth well below zero? Do your debts loom so large that you can't even see the horizon, let alone past it? There is hope. Your debts may determine *when* you serve, and even *where* you serve. But they can never determine *who* you serve.

Whoever you are, wherever you're at, now is the time to listen to Jesus' terrible financial advice.

Notes

1. Merriam-Webster.com. s.v. "terrible," http://merriam-webster.com/dictionary/terrible.

2. David Van Biema and Jeff Chu, "Does God Want You To Be Rich?," *Time*, September 10, 2006, http://content.time.com/time/magazine/article/0,9171,1533448,00.html.

3. From *The Autobiography of Benjamin Franklin*, section eighteen, https://en.wikisource.org/wiki/The_Autobiography_of_Benjamin_Franklin/Section_Eighteen.

4. Vera Bergengruen, "Pope Shuns Limo, Rides in Tiny Fiat," *Miami Herald*, September 22, 2015, http://www.miamiherald.com/news/nation-world/national/article36226770.html; The Hard Times Staff, "Pope Chats Up Fans Gathered Outside Sermon in Hopes of Finding Floor to Crash On," The Hard Times, September 27, 2015, http://thehardtimes.net/2015/09/27/pope-chats-up-fans-gathered-outside-sermon-in-hopes-of-finding-floor-to-crash-on/.

5. T. J. Stanley and W. D. Danko, *The Millionaire Next Door: The Surprising Secrets of America's Wealthy* (New York: RosettaBooks, 1996), 9.

6. See Jennie L. Phipps, "Running out of Money Scares Most People More Than Dying," Bankrate.com, July 7, 2010, http://www.bankrate.com/financing/retirement/running-out-of-money-scares-most-people-more-than-dying/; and also, Catey Hill, "Older People Fear This More Than Death," MarketWatch, July 21, 2016, http://www.marketwatch.com/story/older-people-fear-this-more-than-death-2016-07-18.

7. From *The Journals of Jim Elliot*, ed. Elisabeth Elliot (Grand Rapids: Revell, 1978), 174. http://www2.wheaton.edu/bgc/archives/faq/20.htm

8. Randy Alcorn, *The Treasure Principle: Unlocking the Secret to Joyful Giving* (Colorado Springs: Multnomah Books, 2001), 18.

9. Matt Vande Bunte, "Study Reveals Church Giving at Lowest Point Since Great Depression," *MLive*, October 23, 2010, http://www.mlive.com/living/grand-rapids/index.ssf/2010/10/study_reveals_church_giving_at.html.

10. "Honor Code," U.S. Air Force Academy, http://www.academyadmissions.com/the-experience/character/honor-code/.

11. "The Fraud Triangle," Association of Certified Fraud Examiners, http://www.acfe.com/fraud-triangle.aspx. Concept originally from Donald R. Cressey, *Other People's Money* (Montclair: Patterson Smith, 1973), 30.

12. Merriam-Webster.com, s.v. "terrible," http://merriam-webster.com/dictionary/terrible.

Acknowledgments

Thank you, Dad (Glen), for a hundred walks and a thousand talks. Thank you, Mom (Nancy), for loving God and loving me. Thanks to L.P. and Bobbi Leung, for your commitment to Christian accounting ethics in honor of your son Timothy.

This book is a lifetime of thoughts, so I owe thanks as much to those who have long since gone on ahead to that "great cloud of witnesses" as to those still with us. Like Eleanor Schwab, a pastor's wife who challenged kids to memorize God's Word and extended her gnarled hands to everyone, despite the pain. To John Mitchell, a then eighty-year-old professor and founder of Multnomah School of the Bible, who challenged us to read our Bibles and fall in love with the Savior. To Pastor Dave Bechtel, who for over a decade has faithfully challenged his congregation to regularly read God's Word. And thanks to the many friends and family for the memories and moments filled with good questions and great thoughts too numerous to include in one short book. So to all those who love the God who delights in kindness, justice, and righteousness, to Him be the glory.

Finally, thanks to John Trent, mentor, David Van Diest, agent, and the Moody Publishers Team, especially Connor Sterchi, coordinating editor, and John Hinkley, associate publisher of the Gary Chapman Team, for believing in this book.

About the Author

John Thornton is the L.P. and Bobbi Leung Chair of Accounting Ethics at Azusa Pacific University, a Christian university with over ten thousand students near Los Angeles, California, where he chairs the L.P. and Timothy Leung School of Accounting, and oversees a $15 million endowment for accounting ethics and education. He teaches accounting ethics and forensic accounting, and speaks nationally on equipping the church to master money. His research on accounting ethics has been published in several academic journals. He has served as Chair of the American Accounting Association's *Public Interest Section*, Chair of the AAA's *Professionalism and Ethics Committee*, and held senior leadership positions at Washington State University and the U.S. Air Force Academy. Dr. Thornton is a CPA with a Ph.D. in Accounting from Washington State University. He is married to Alyssa, with sons Joshua, Benjamin, and Jacob. Visit John's website at gettingrichright.com.

IS YOUR CAREER ALL IT COULD BE?

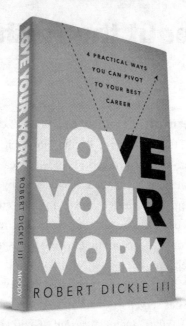

Whether you're just starting out, looking for a change, or experiencing unwanted change, there's a way forward. *Love Your Work* is about pivoting step-by-step to a more satisfying career. It will help you:

- Dream up bigger goals than you have now—and meet them
- Search out new careers or niches within your industry
- Pursue work and success holistically

ALSO AVAILABLE AS AN EBOOK

From the Word to Life®